To. Jan

Have many good
days this season!

Neil W Graesser

14 · 3 · 90

FLY FISHING FOR SALMON

River Orchy by Bridge of Orchy

FLY FISHING FOR SALMON

Neil Graesser

THE BOYDELL PRESS
STONE WALL PRESS

First published 1982
by The Boydell Press
an imprint of Boydell & Brewer Ltd
PO Box 9 Woodbridge Suffolk IP12 3DF
Reprinted 1987

British Library Cataloguing in Publication Data

Graesser, Neil
Fly fishing for salmon.
1. Salmon-fishing   2. Fly fishing
I. Title
799.1'7555   SH685
ISBN 0-85115-172-8

Printed by St Edmundsbury Press Ltd, Bury St Edmunds, Suffolk

CONTENTS

List of illustrations

List of diagrams

Introduction

I was born in the Vale of Llangollen very close to the banks of the Welsh Dee. My father owned a stretch of the Dee and soon afterwards he also bought an estate in Sutherland with the fishing on the Lower Cassley.

My father was a keen fisherman and largely as a result of his help and advice I was lucky enough to catch my first salmon at the age of six. From then on I became a fanatical fisherman and when I was young I literally spent every moment available to me on the banks of a river, quite regardless of whether the conditions were favourable or not. I soon found that my interest in fishing extended to my quarry and I started a lifelong study into the natural history of both trout and salmon and their environment.

This has led me into fishery management and I now work as a consultant advising particularly on the protection and conservation of salmon stocks and the improvement of the angling potential of many rivers.

My work has given me the experience of fishing on many of the salmon rivers of Scotland and I have spent many, many peaceful hours in intense enjoyment pitting my wits against one of the most unpredictable quarries in the world during which time I have been lucky enough to kill several thousand of these wonderfully sporting fish.

This book is written as an attempt to repay a small part of the debt that I owe to fishing.

I have written about fly fishing for salmon only. And although the vast majority of the fish that I have caught have been caught on the fly, I do not on this account wish to appear to be wholly committed to fly fishing. I have caught salmon on every lure available, but I do believe that catching a salmon on the fly is the best and by far the most enjoyable way. I hope that what I say will be of interest to all fishermen, especially anyone starting to fish, of whom my son is one.

Rosehall, 1982

Fly Fishing for Salmon: Why and How

Although this whole book is about fly fishing for salmon, there are only two occasions when the angler is really trying to attract a salmon to a fly. The first is when he is fishing with a dry fly, and the second is when he is trailing his fly on the surface of the water either 'dibbling' or loch fishing. It is important to realise this because I maintain that the fisherman who knows precisely what he is trying to imitate and why, will catch far more fish than the one who just fishes and hopes.

I think at the outset it is best to consider the life of the salmon while it is in the sea, after it has migrated as a smolt, a mere 5 or 6 inches in length. Even if that smolt stays but 12 months in salt water, it will return the next summer as a grilse averaging 5–6 lbs in weight. Grilse from the heavier strains of fish can weigh much more and 12–14 lb fish have been recorded, whereas at the beginning of the grilse run the forerunners weigh a mere 1½–3 lbs. But as an average its growth rate is phenomenal. To achieve this the salmon must turn itself into the most voracious predator, feeding on the small fish of the sea such as elvers, sand eels and sprats, and plankton.

There was a theory which held that salmon migrated to the Sargasso Sea and fed on elvers as they drifted over in the Gulf Stream. This theory convincingly explained why salmon took a small fly in warm water and a large fly in cold water. Whereas the first part of this theory is definitely wrong the second part is probably right because we now know that salmon from many different countries of origin feed in the northern hemisphere off Greenland, and this area is now acknowledged to be one of the major feeding grounds for the species. Therefore there is little doubt that salmon migrating to this area use the numerous warm and cold water current systems that are to be found in this part of the Atlantic Ocean, to assist them on their journey to

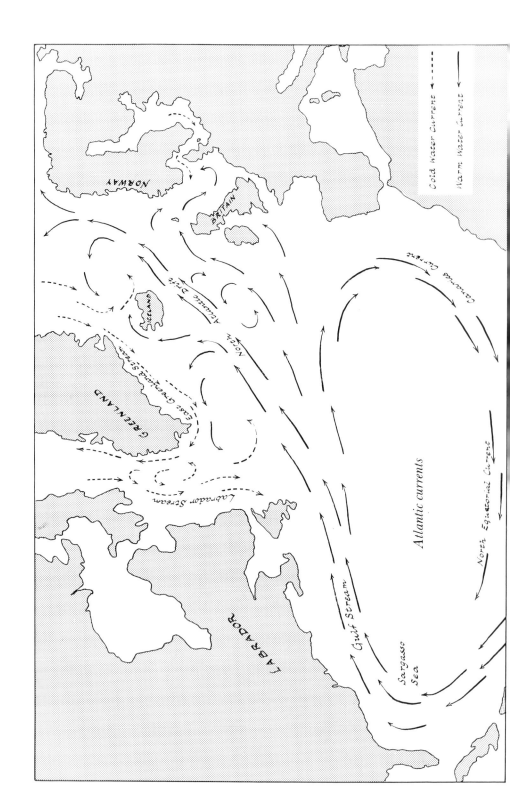

Atlantic currents

Cold Water Current ←----
Warm Water Current ←——

NORWAY

BRITAIN

ICELAND

GREENLAND

North Atlantic Drift

East Greenland Stream

Labrador Stream

LABRADOR

Gulf Stream

Sargasso
Sea

North Equatorial Current

Canaries Current

and from these feeding grounds. The current known as the North Atlantic drift will be followed not only by salmon migrating to their feeding grounds from Europe and Scandinavia but also by *leptocephalus*, pre-elver stage eels and elvers on their journey from the Sargasso Sea to their feeding grounds in the fresh water rivers and lakes in the same countries. It is, therefore, extremely likely that salmon feed on these creatures when their paths cross.

We do know that salmon feed at sea on small fish such as capelin, sand eels, the smaller members of the crustacea such as crill and plankton. It may well be that the reason that salmon take small flies in warmer water temperatures and larger flies in colder water temperatures is directly attributable to their memory of the type and size of food that was available to them in these warm and cold current systems of the ocean.

The other thing to consider is the vexed question of whether salmon feed or do not feed on their return to fresh water. My own view is entirely pragmatic. Salmon do not need to feed in fresh water and no doubt many salmon do not feed. If they did, given the barren habitat of most Scottish rivers, and the size of the fish concerned, they would turn into cannibals and of necessity rapidly devour their own species to the point of extinction. Therefore to enable the species to continue nature has provided the salmon with the ability to forego food while in fresh water and live on its accumulated fat. It is worth noting that in the old days it was said that the salmon from the large east coast rivers in Scotland the Spey, Dee, Tay and Tweed fetched higher prices at the fishmongers than salmon from the north or west coast rivers, because these fish had generally many more miles to travel up river to reach their spawning grounds and therefore entered the river with a larger store of accumulated fat which meant they were better eating. In actual fact this is fallacy, the real reason for the higher price was that these rivers were closer to the main transport routes and markets.

But, and I maintain this through thick and thin, while nature makes this provision, it does not take away from the salmon all memory of former feeding patterns. Every year salmon will be seen rising at mayflies on the Test, and I have seen them doing so in Highland rivers that have a hatch of *ephemera danica*, surely a memory of when they fed on these tasty morsels as parr. Every year salmon are caught on prawns and worms, and if you catch a salmon on a worm you will often find the hook far down in its stomach. In the case of the prawn, this is triggered off by memory of eating crustacea in the sea, and a worm will either be

5

the memory of worms consumed when the salmon was a parr in the same waters, or lobworms may well resemble some small octopus or squid-like creature. And every year salmon, innumerable salmon, are caught on so-called flies and minnows which resemble small fish, waterborne invertebrates or plankton, and the impulse to take these objects is triggered by some dormant feeding pattern from the fish's past. This to me seems reasonable and logical.

I know there are many who will say, why then is nothing ever found in a salmon's stomach in fresh water. Well first of all I would be very surprised if very much was found but the number of people who dissect the stomach of every fish they catch is very small. Secondly the digestive juices of a salmon's stomach are extremely strong. Many times I have caught salmon on a worm and because the fish was hooked so far down its stomach I have cut my line rather than struggled to extract the hook. Whenever I have gutted these fish, generally after only a few hours I have found not only no trace of the worms but the thread binding the worm hook to the trace has been dissolved, or partially dissolved and rotted. And finally nearly every salmon excretes a brown substance from its vent, which would indicate to me that the fish has eaten something sometime.

And it follows from this that when the angler is fishing with a fly, he is really imitating a small fish, and when, in the summer, he is fishing properly with a floating line and hanging his fly in the current, he is imitating plankton.

Having said that, and I am well aware that not everyone will agree with it, I think that the angler should next think about the salmon, its eyesight, and what it sees as it lies in the river. If you consider the set of the eyes on a salmon's head you will realise that at no time except at extreme vision, can a salmon focus both eyes on the same object. In other words, a salmon can see two things perfectly clearly at the one time. A fly that is hung directly over its head is practically invisible as it is at the extreme extent of vision of either eye and the same applies to an object just in front of its nose. This does not mean that salmon have not the keenest vision and superb accuracy of judgement. They have. But there is no doubt whatsoever that a fly crossing a pool away from a fish is much more attractive to it, and far more likely to be taken than the fly coming towards it. And this is the typical behaviour of a predator.

The next thing to consider is the view that the salmon has from its lie. Much the clearest view that the fish can have is against the sky whether the day is dark or not, and the only exception to this is when the sun is shining directly down the pool, when any fish looking directly into it would be blinded. Therefore, and I cover this point in more detail in the chapters on spring and summer fishing, it makes sense *initially* to fish your fly high in the water, which gives the fish the greatest chance to see it clearly. Once you sink your fly closer to the fish it must be viewed through a wall of water which may be turbid, against the rocks, bank, vegetation and bed of the river and it cannot possibly be as visible to the fish.

The other great advantage of keeping your fly close to the surface is that you are making the fish come up to it and therefore you are far more likely to hook him, because of necessity he will be travelling faster, and also if he misses the fly you will invariably see some sign or boil on the surface and can try that fish again, which you will not if the fly is at any depth. This in a way is a digression from my main point but I believe that it is very important and something which many fishermen do not really think about.

If we accept everything I have said then it follows that, generally, what we as fishermen are trying to do, is to imitate a small fish and stimulate the feeding memory of the salmon. It is a fact that the temperature of the water directly controls the size of fly that a salmon will take. When the water temperature is below 42°F then you have to fish with a fly of 2 inches or over; between 42–50°F, salmon can be caught on a large variety of sizes of fly from 6-inch tubes in high water conditions down to ¼-inch, and once the water temperature rises over 50°F then you are far more likely to catch salmon on small flies, say from size 7 downwards, except in a very high river. It is perhaps worth noting that water temperature does not have the same effect on baits, such as worms and prawns, but these are not really so effective until the water temperature rises over 40°F.

I do firmly believe that generally in the summer most people fish with flies that are too big but I must admit that in the last few years the long tailed variety of flies, as large as 2½ inches, such as the Blue Elverin, Munro Killer, Collie Dog and Tadpole, have become much more popular and I have killed fish on them in the summer months when I would normally fish with a fly size 10. It seems probable therefore that these imitate some sea creature which can be found in a large variety of water temperatures.

Now turning back to what you as an angler are trying to imitate. The first thing is to try and give your lure as life-like an appearance in the water as possible. Many anglers simply cast out their fly and let it traverse the width of the pool without touching their line until it comes across to their side of the river when they handline to make the fly buoyant before recasting. This I think is wrong. If you fish like this you are first of all allowing the fly to find its own depth and secondly you are relying on the currents and eddies present in any pool to put life into your fly. If you make a bad cast and there are few of us who don't the fly will submerge and then the current will grip the sunken line and drag the fly across the pool too fast. At times the fly, at the mercy of the current will sink back in the water, and as it hits eddies it will twist and turn unnaturally, or even fall away suddenly.

I firmly believe that flies fished like this are not only less attractive to fish but because of their jerky and unpredictable motion are far more difficult for any interested fish to intercept and many a taking fish can be missed for this reason.

Other fishermen cast beautifully at a 45° angle downstream, and some even further downstream, and you can watch them with pleasure as they cover each pool in even rhythmical fashion but if you fish like this you won't, in my opinion, catch the greatest number of fish. The reason for this is that if you are a perfect caster and cast at this angle, everything will land in a straight line and the fly will start to traverse the pool immediately it hits the water. Therefore any fish lying near where the fly lands really has very little chance to see and size up the fly before it starts to fish away from him, and I maintain that a number of fish will be missed by anglers who fish in this way.

The best method is to cast at 60° across the river, ugly though it may look and, immediately the fly hits the water, move your rod square to the current and handline two pulls of 18 inches each. Then whether you are fishing fast current or not, keep handlining about 6 inches per pull at the same time easing your rod tip downstream to lead your fly in its traverse of the pool. When you have led your fly into the near edge of the pool you should move your rod tip out towards the centre of the river and at the same time handline in fairly fast to make it buoyant before recasting.

If you do this carefully you will catch many fish that are lying right in on your bank which otherwise would not be attracted to the fly dangled over their nose and then drawn very swiftly away as you lift your line to recast.

There are several reasons for fishing like this. By casting at 60° your fly will of necessity hesitate for a moment before it starts to fish across the pool, the squaring of your rod and the two initial draws will iron out any kinks that the current develops in your line and puts you in direct touch with your fly. At the same time it will keep the fly buoyant near the surface and each subsequent draw on the line will impart a darting lifelike motion to the fly, as if it was a small fish moving in short bursts. You are therefore constantly in touch with your fly and in a position to strike directly you feel the fish.

Depending on the type of fly you are using you can fish a pool faster or slower, and it often pays if two are fishing a pool together for one angler to adopt one form of presentation and the second a different one. One method which I use a lot myself is backing up which has a chapter on its own, but it is worth saying a few words here about different water heights and different flies.

If you are fishing with one of the long-tailed flies then I think it should be fished fairly quickly as the speed of movement through the water makes the tail quiver in a lifelike manner. One of the old-fashioned salmon flies, a Yellow Eagle, had a prominent hackle at its throat and if this fly was fished with a quick jerky action, this hackle opened and shut in a very lifelike manner and I have known it take fish on days when other very similar patterns such as the Yellow Torrish or Garry Dog proved useless.

Another way to vary your presentation is to cast even squarer across the pool and strip your fly even faster across the current and it is always worth trying this if you have risen a fish which then doesn't take you or will not look at another pattern presented in a more traditional manner. However in low water conditions in the spring and in the summer when the water warms up you should cut down the speed at which you fish your fly. In low water conditions it pays to fish your fly at about half the pace I have described and in the summer months you must give the fish plenty of time to size up your fly. Remember that as the water temperature rises so salmon become more lethargic and you must give them every opportunity to make a mistake.

Finally in the summer you can choose to fish the orthodox method of greased line fishing as advocated by the late A. G. Wood and imitate plankton instead of a small fish or waterborne invertebrate. This, if it is to be successful, must be a conscious decision, because you are now not trying to imitate something swimming across the current but an inert creature hanging in the stream. Plankton is a vegetation which hangs in suspension in the water therefore in order to imitate it you must simulate this action. This means you must prevent your fly being dragged by the current at any time during its traverse across the pool. To start with you must cast downstream at an angle of 45° and as soon as your fly lands mend your line across the current in order that the line and fly maintain a course as parallel to the water flow as possible. If at any time your line begins to drag your fly then you must remend your line to prevent this, and it may be necessary to mend your line several times in one cast as your fly traverses the width of the pool. In this case when the salmon takes you must give him time before you strike because of necessity you are not in direct contact with your fly. Personally I only fish like this when the traditional methods have failed me but it is worth trying as another weapon in the salmon fisher's armoury.

Tackle

The first item of tackle that any salmon fisher must possess is a rod and nowadays there is a large variety available both of size and material. Therefore any advice that I can give on the best or most suitable rod must be tempered according to the type of fishing that you generally do, the rivers that you fish on and the time of the year that you fish.

Rods nowadays are made from split cane, which can be spliced or jointed, fibre-glass or carbon fibre. Wooden rods made from split cane are the heaviest but many people prefer them, with carbon fibre rods being the most modern, the lightest and the most expensive. However for a beginner a number of the fibre-glass rods which are generally cheaper than the other two, are light and perfectly adequate and I think I would advise a beginner to get one of these initially until he or she has had the opportunity of trying out a number of different types of rod and establishes a personal preference. As to length a 13 or 14 foot rod is generally adequate for most purposes and will be suitable for most rivers and seasons of the year.

If, however, you are planning to fish, or you do fish, for a large part of the year on a variety of rivers, then I would buy two or three rods so that I had a number which would give me the optimum performance on a variety of rivers. Among them would be a 15 or 16 foot carbon fibre rod for use on large rivers and during the spring and a 12 foot rod for summer fishing of carbon fibre or split cane. I think the smaller split cane rods are very good but the larger ones unless you are lucky and get a good one tend to be a bit flabby in their centre section. Alternatively, if you don't like carbon fibre rods you will need a stiff 14 or 15 foot rod for the earlier part of the year and you can either buy a fibre-glass one or attend a sale of old fishing rods where you may be

Salmon fishing at dusk on the Spey

lucky enough to pick up an old spliced Greenheart or steel centred split cane rod of this length.

Both these types of rod to my mind have the bone and force that modern rods lack but they are heavier and much harder work to fish with.

Once you have your rod you must then get a reel and it is essential that you get a reel which balances your rod. Most modern reels are made from light alloy and they are definitely not heavy enough to balance, say, an old-fashioned Greenheart spliced rod. There is nothing worse than fishing with a rod that is tip heavy and again if you have an old-fashioned salmon rod, scour the country until you find an old reel that is heavy enough to balance it. Many of these reels are still about, with sufficient care they will last for a lifetime, and they have the other priceless advantage that their drums are usually large enough to contain 100+ yards of backing. And if you fish on big river systems such as the Spey or go to Norway then you must have at least this amount of backing on your reel.

Modern reels are perfectly heavy enough for modern carbon fibre and fibre-glass rods but do make sure that you buy one with a big enough drum to take all the backing you require.

The next thing you need is a line and here I think you must be very careful and consider your rod, your abilities as a caster, and the type of fishing that you will do. If you are fishing in the early spring then you must have a full sinking line. My own preference is for a slow sinker, although a fast sinking line is all right if you are only going to fish one of the big rivers such as the Tweed, Tay or Spey. Get a line that is a minimum of 30 yards in length and ensure that it is double tapered. Double tapered lines take up much less room on the reel, they are easier to cast, and when one end is worn you can double the life of your line by reversing it.

Some people I know feel that a floating line with a sinking tip is adequate. My own firm opinion is that for early spring fishing that is not the case. The floating part of the line creates a buoyancy which definitely narrows the depth range at which you can fish your fly and I would only advocate its use by the elderly, a disabled angler and some women, who will find the floating line easier to lift off the water.

If you are fishing in the late spring or summer then you will also need a full floating line. Some fishermen I know carry two rods one with a floating line and one with a sunk line so that they can switch easily from one to the other as conditions dictate and there are some modern reels which have interchangeable drums which can be loaded with different types of lines. And there are occasions and rivers when it can be an advantage to fish a floating line with a sinking tip – I will deal with this in a minute.

But whatever the type of line you require you must get one that balances your rod. Modern rods are precision made and will only 'work' with the correct weight of line. Generally the makers will recommend the weight of line that should be used for the rod and to start with I would firmly recommend that you get the heaviest weight of line recommended for your rod. Tournament or professional casters are capable of throwing a much longer line than the average angler and therefore they will use a light weight of line on a rod, say 13 foot in length. If a beginner gets this weight of line on say a carbon fibre rod, they will find it almost impossible to cast any length of line at all. So to start with get the heaviest line recommended for your rod, take advice from your tackle dealer, who certainly should be competent to advise you, and as you become more proficient and can cast a longer line then you can change to a lighter line.

One tip on new lines which is worth knowing. The modern salmon line has a plastic finish on a nylon core and is definitely resilient to bad usage. However when you buy a line you will find that it is wound on a spindle in a box. After you have spliced the line onto the backing you will find that your line is kinky and if you wind it directly onto your reel and just start fishing the new line will kink and jam in the bottom rung of your rod as you cast. This is not only extremely irritating but will crack the plastic finish of the line and shorten its life. To prevent this, the first time you use a new line go into a field, pay all the line off your rod, right down to the backing and then walk at least a hundred yards through the field trailing your line behind you. This allows the whole length of the line to uncurl and when you wind it back onto the reel you will find that you have no more trouble, and it certainly lengthens the life of your line by an incredible amount.

I would say that if you only wanted to purchase one line for the whole season then you should buy a slow sinking line, for now it is possible to buy special grease for plastic lines which will not damage the coating and therefore you can convert such a line into a floating line for summer fishing. Personally I use a full floating line in the summer but full floating lines have one disadvantage which can be overcome by using a floating line with a sinking tip. If you are fishing a river which has a number of glassy 'draws' then you may find with a nylon cast, a light tube fly and a floating line, that your fly will not keep just below the surface, but come skittering to the top. A sinking tip is one way of overcoming this. Generally I feel, however, that sinking tips cause the fly to sink too deeply in the summer, though there are anglers I know who overcome this by shortening the sinking part of the line, and rebalancing the line with a heavy nylon collar between the line and the fine nylon point. Personally in spite of all the instant attractions of modern fly lines, fast sinking, slow sinking, floating, sinking tip, they are not in my opinion the equal of the old dressed silk Kingfisher lines, and I am only sorry they are not manufactured any longer.

The last piece of casting equipment you will need is nylon. It is very important that you aim for the correct balance between the weight of nylon you use for otherwise the fly will not extend properly at the end of your cast. This is particularly true if too light a weight of nylon is used with a heavy fly. If the nylon does not lead the fly out correctly everything will land in a heap and this can cause inadvertent knots in your cast which can cause a break when you are playing a fish.

Personally, in the spring, I just use a level 9 foot cast of 25–30 lbs breaking strain in high water conditions and I reduce this to 20 lbs when the water is low. I find that nylon of these weights is stiff enough to lead my fly out perfectly adequately. If however you want to taper your cast then either plait a collar of heavy nylon and attach a short length of this to your line and then add a leader of nylon to the collar, or attach a length of 35 lbs breaking strain nylon to your line and taper your cast down to 25 lbs breaking strain at the point.

I never use nylon of less than 20 lbs breaking strain until I reduce my fly size below 1½ inches. And I would continue to use nylon of that weight if I was fishing in a very rocky, rough river. In normal rivers I would, in late spring and in high water in summer, use nylon of 18 lbs breaking strain, although if I was fishing a very big river with big pools, few hazards and little likelihood of a hooked fish leaving the pool, I would reduce this to 14–15 lbs breaking strain.

In the summer in very low water when you are fishing with very small flies you have to reduce the breaking strain again and you can go as light as 8 lbs. I wouldn't recommend going any finer and remember that nylon manufacturers are constantly improving the quality and strength of nylon so that modern 10–12 lbs breaking strain nylon is probably the equivalent in thickness to an 8 lbs breaking strain of some years ago. A small fly swum on too heavy a cast will not behave properly and will either drag in the water or swim in a crabwise fashion. Similarly try to get nylon that is as stiff as possible – supple nylon tends to crinkle, is bad for knotting and lacks the bone to lead the fly out properly. Also if you are using a dropper with very supple nylon, it inevitably gets entangled in the main cast.

The only trouble with nylon is that it does not last for ever and it deteriorates if it is stored at too high a temperature or exposed to excessive light. It is well worth considering replacing all your stock of nylon each year, even a complete range is not vastly expensive and if by so doing you save yourself one unnecessary break then I feel the investment both in money and gained pleasure is well worth while.

Finally flies. If you are going to fish throughout the whole year you will of necessity require a large number of different patterns, different types and different sizes of fly. But if you give some thought to the matter you can purchase wisely and thereby cut down your expense. Tube flies are the least expensive type of fly if they are well made and unless they are lost last for many years mainly because they do not have to be discarded if the hooks are broken and, unless they are damaged by battering against hard objects in the backcast, are seldom damaged themselves. If you see the binding at the head of a tube fly becoming damaged put this fly aside and either repair it yourself or get a friend to rebind it and revarnish it which makes it as good as new. Otherwise if you continue to fish with a fly in this condition you will eventually end up with a bare tube.

For spring fishing ordinary tube flies are normally found in a limited variety of patterns. Black and orange, black and yellow, black, yellow and red and Hairy Mary's are amongst the most popular. The long tailed varieties such as the Collie and Tadpole are also very effective on many rivers. All these can be dressed on aluminium, brass or polythene tubes, and the body of the tube can be dressed or undressed. It is purely a matter of preference. Personally I prefer the tube to have a top wing only leaving the underside open in order to show off the body of the tube, which can be dressed or undressed. Provided you have these six varieties in sizes from 1 inch to 4 inches you will literally have a sufficient range of this type of fly to cover all spring conditions.

In this selection you can find a pattern that is effective in any light and that covers the old dark, silver and bright varieties of the old authentic patterned flies. If you want to use traditional flies in the spring the best known in the dark range are the Black Doctor, the Thunder and Lightning, the Jock Scott, the Childers, the Akroyd: in the silver range, the Dusty Miller, Mar Lodge, Silver Doctor, Haslam and Silver Grey and in the bright range, the Yellow and Red Torrish, Green Highlander, Garry Dog, and Gordon. There are, of course many, many other patterns, but they would cost you a fortune to purchase and they are easily broken. Probably the weakest part of the tube flies range are the silver flies but amateur fly tiers can make a silver tube fly to his own pattern. Personally I view silver bodied flies as probably the most effective of all, but it is often sufficient to fish with tubes dressed on aluminium with the body exposed.

Summer patterns of tube flies revolve round the Stoat's Tail and Hairy Mary and many fly tiers produce their own special adaptations. Size does not really matter for provided you have the smallest sizes you need from ¼ inch upwards you can build these up to any size by putting more than one on at the same time with equal success. The only drawback about these smaller varieties of tube fly is that the treble cannot be stabilised as it can in the bigger variety by using either rubber or polythene sleeves attached to the end of the tube into which the eye of the treble can be drawn. The loose treble on the small tubes very often shoots ahead of the fly in the forward cast and can often hook back on the cast above the fly which ruins that particular cast. On a windy day this can become a nuisance as on many occasions you can fish for an appreciable time after this has happened without being aware of the fact.

The Waddington type fly is another useful invention. Although slightly more expensive than ordinary tube flies they are dressed in a greater variety of patterns and many of the old patterned flies are to be found duplicated on the Waddington type of shank. However, if a hook of the treble is broken it is not easy to replace without damaging the fly.

The third type of fly is the authentic single or double hooked fly. These are expensive but it is really necessary to have a selection of those particularly in the small sizes as they have a decided advantage over the other types of flies in certain conditions. They are that much heavier than tube flies and sit the water better especially when you are using a greased or floating line in a fast flowing river. In recent years Colonel Esmond Drury has produced many authentic patterns dressed on heavy long-shanked trebles and these also can be most effective particularly on faster flowing rivers.

I think myself that you are better to make certain rules about patterns and stick to them. My own rule is to cover the traditional, dark, bright and silver shades and then make sure that I have every available size in a few patterns that I am likely to need. But maybe I am wrong. I do think it is very important to have a large variety of fly sizes to choose from for as I say in the chapter on *Choosing a Fly* I think size is much more important than pattern. But I know that I fish a great deal and I think that experience makes you conservative in this respect. Therefore if you want to collect a variety of flies then do so and maybe one day it will be that one fly that the salmon will take and no other and you will be the only lucky angler.

As to knots, again I am an unashamed conservative. I find the half-blood knot much the most serviceable, particularly for attaching the treble of a tube fly to the nylon. I use five twists and then pass the end of the nylon back through the eye of the treble and loop of the nylon at the same time. If you do this then the end of the nylon lies flat down the shank of the treble and does not stick out at right angles. I also use the half-blood knot for small flies and Esmond Drury flies but for larger flies I prefer the old figure-of-eight knot. For attaching the cast to the line again I use a figure-of-eight knot although other people either splice a loop in the line which you can then pass the loop of the cast through or if you want you can attach a thick length of nylon to your line with a needle knot. This is rather a bore to do but it does have the advantage that the line and nylon are a continuous line without the interruptions of any knots. To make a loop in a cast I merely double the cast and pass the end through the loop twice and I find that this very seldom lets me down.

Once again I cannot stress too greatly the importance of balance between rod, reel, line cast and fly as the most important thing when you equip yourself for fly fishing. Many anglers wrongly blame a rod for their bad performance when it is only the wrong type of line that is the problem. When in doubt take the best advice that is available to make sure that everything is balanced properly. Even the most experienced of anglers cannot make a good job without a proper balance.

Casting

It is obvious that the ability of an angler to cast a reasonable length of line under any conditions is the single most important fact in salmon fishing, indeed without this ability the angler is unlikely to achieve any great success. Having said that I would also say that the rudiments of casting are easily learnt and that modern salmon rods, particularly those of fibre-glass and carbon fibre construction, and modern lines, reduce the effort required and make casting relatively easy, even for old ladies and young boys, far, far, easier and less tiring than the heavy Greenheart and split cane rods used a generation ago.

Now if you are a complete beginner how do you start? Certainly I wouldn't start by trying to learn from a book but it may be a help if I outline in this chapter those elements in casting a salmon fly that are important because it may help you, if you are a beginner, to assimilate the advice you will be given more easily.

First of all find an instructor – ideally one with a river available – but the instructor is more important, initially, than the river. With the large numbers of people taking up salmon fishing each year there are a number of casting schools distributed around the country where the beginner can get expert tuition and pick up the rudiments of casting in a very short space of time. It is a good way to learn. However, if you don't want to do that, you will no doubt have a friend with experience. Go to him or her and ask for help. Make sure that you have a rod with a line that balances it, for particularly with modern rods as I have outlined in the chapter on tackle, this is an essential.

Then, assuming that you have no river available go to the nearest flat field or lawn and start there. A salmon rod, indeed any rod is an instrument designed to throw a line some distance across water. Its design has been refined over the years and it is a tough efficient piece

Normal cast

of equipment provided it isn't abused. So the first thing you as a beginner must learn is not to be frightened of it, it won't fly apart in your hands however delicate it looks. The second thing is that in order to throw your line forwards you must first pull it backwards, and then allow your line time to straighten out behind you. It is a form of applied mechanics. As in all sports efficiency comes with practice and timing, but you will find casting easier if you remember that the line must be pulled – out of the water or off the field wherever you are – allowed to straighten out behind you and then pushed forward.

First of all you must stand comfortably with your feet apart and, assuming that you are right handed, with your left foot slightly in front of your right. Hold the rod with your right hand near the top of the cork grip on your rod and the left hand in between the butt and the reel. Pull off some line and then lift the rod sharply backwards with enough impetus to throw the line out behind you, count 1, 2, and then push the rod forwards with your right hand only. It is almost impossible to describe the action of casting in words, but there are various tips that will help the beginner. First of all practically every beginner and a good few fishermen who count themselves experienced, take the rod too far back. It should only just go past the vertical and if you can try and think of stopping it in the vertical position then the chances are you will get it about right. Secondly I think it helps the beginner if he or she can think of tossing the line up into the air behind them, throw it away from you. If your back cast is right and the line is fully extended behind you, then the chances are everything will be all right when it goes out in front, and if you can consciously think in those terms then that will help. Another fault is keeping your hands too low when you cast. I know that you will see many ghillies and expert fishermen casting with no perceptible movement of the hands, above the waist, whistling out the most immaculate and seemingly effortless lines. But when you are starting try to get your left hand, assuming you are right handed, up under your chin. This forces you to lift the rod properly. Another fault you see with beginners is a pronounced swing of the body when they cast. Anyone moving their body is trying to get their body to throw the line across the river. Very difficult – indeed impossible. The rod has been designed to do this and you will help it by keeping your body as still as possible. If you are fishing in a river with a ghillie watch him cast, the chances are that only his arms and hands will move and if you find that your back is tired after a day's fishing it is a sure sign that you have been guilty of this fault.

If you have a tutor then he can help you to overcome most of these faults. I would advocate placing a hand behind the pupil's shoulder which will soon teach him not to take the rod too far back, and counting as the cast is made which will help the beginner to realise that he has more time than he thinks. Generally casting should be effortless, an activity which in itself provides immense pleasure but such skill will only come with practice.

Once you have learnt to throw a line some distance then you must learn to shoot line. This means that you either pull in some of the line you have cast, or pull some more line off your reel so that it lies on the ground at your feet and you then trap your line with the forefinger of your top hand when you lift your rod to make your backcast. When you push the rod forward you let go of this line as your line begins to lead forward in the air in front of you and before it touches the water, or the field, wherever you happen to be practising. The timing of this release is important and the common fault is to let go of your line too early. Delay as long as you can. Again with practice you will find that you gain more proficiency at this and an expert can shoot up to 10 yards of line. The reasons that this is so important are twofold. First of all it enables you to cast a longer line. A rod is only capable of handling a certain weight of line into the air and if you can shoot 5 or 6 yards of line you can increase your casting distance by this amount. Secondly, particularly if you are fishing with a sunk line in the spring, you must work your fly up to the surface each time you recast.

If you don't, at worst you won't be able to get your line out of the water, and in addition you are imposing a severe strain on the centre joint of your rod. The way to do this is to handline in when your fly comes round below you and raise the tip of your rod to an angle of about 60°.

If you are starting out on dry land it is impossible to simulate this but your tutor must teach you to handline before recasting. It is the main disadvantage of trying to learn to cast on land, the other disadvantage is that grass does not create the same resistance as water and therefore you cannot pull back your line with the same snap as you can when fishing running water. You have to use more force but if you don't have a river to practise on you are better to practise in a field or on a lawn than not at all. Now if you are lucky and have a river in front of you for your first lesson, get your tutor to take you to a pool with an even stream, with a rod and line that balance one another and a floating line. The reason for the floating line is that it is much easier

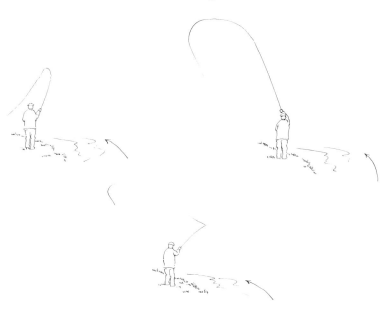

Back-handed cast

to lift off the water and there is less danger of the line becoming drowned when you come to recast.

When talking about a river you always describe the banks as if you were looking downstream. Thus when you are fishing the left bank the correct shoulder to fish off is the right one and vice versa. As most people are right handed most people would fish from the left bank of a river given a choice. You will find if you have been casting on a lawn that casting in a river with moving water is easier, and that you will be able to lift your line off with less effort. The only thing to watch initially is that you have enough room for your backcast and that there are no obstacles for your fly to catch on behind you.

When I am teaching people to cast very often I teach them to cast over their left hand shoulder using the grip as if they were casting over their right shoulder. My reason for this is that this makes it physically impossible for them to take the rod back too far and when they have got into the habit of timing the cast properly then they can revert to casting over the correct shoulder.

When you have mastered the elements of casting and are beginning to throw a reasonable line, try fishing with a sunk line or one with a sinking tip. There is no essential difference between using one of these and a floating line but because they sink deeper in the water you will have to take care to make your fly buoyant by handlining several feet of line in quickly at the end of each cast and/or raising the tip of your rod as I have said.

Once you have got the hang of this then really you should go to the other bank of the river and teach yourself to cast over the other shoulder. When I was a boy I fished on the Welsh Dee, and I started off fishing from the right hand bank over my left shoulder. After a bit my father forbade me to use that bank and decreed that henceforth I should only fish from the left bank. As our stretch of the river was heavily wooded my only chance of covering any water at all was to fish off my right shoulder and at the time I thought such an imposition most unjust. In fact I now bless his wisdom for it made me into a completely ambidextrous fisherman although in moments of severe stress I would, I admit, prefer to fish off my left shoulder. There is no doubt that it is a great advantage to be able to fish off both shoulders with equal facility. If you have to fish off your wrong shoulder in heavily wooded stretches of a river this can be a real disadvantage and also if the wind is upstream, fishing off the wrong shoulder presents the fly at the wrong angle and makes your line bounce off the wind, so to speak, instead of cutting into it.

I know some fishermen who overcome this by casting backhanded but it does mean that you have to reverse your grip on the rod before and after every cast and if you don't your cramped arm action does not allow your fly to traverse the current of the pool properly and this also prevents you from being able to strike so quickly or effectively.

There are a number of casting variations which can help you to overcome adverse conditions, whether they are caused by the weather or the bank behind you. The two most common are the Spey and Double Spey cast and you have to use them if you are fishing a river with banks of trees right up to the water's edge which would catch your fly if it passed behind you. Taking the single Spey or roll cast first, you fish over the same shoulder as you would normally and raising your rod, draw your fly upstream until it is level with and beside you, you then make what I can only describe as a circle with your rod, out, up and over, making a large bight in your line which you roll out into the centre of the river. With a bit of practice, particularly with a downstream wind this is quite an easy cast to make and a most effective one. It is particularly useful not only when you have a difficult bank to cope with, but also when you have a very

24

Single Spey cast

strong downstream wind, when, because the fly never passes behind you, there is no danger of hooking yourself in the back of the neck.

The next cast is the Double Spey and in the hands of the expert this cast is a real delight to watch and it enables the expert to cast a much longer line than the normal overhead cast. To do this you fish over the wrong shoulder. There are three movements: fishing from the right bank you first of all lift the rod so that your fly comes straight up towards you and lies about 5 yards from your feet. Then you swing the rod backhanded over your left shoulder forming a bight of line on the left and then in a figure of eight movement back over your right shoulder, the last movement is a deliberate cut of the rod straight down to the water, and your line will go whistling out as if by magic. I know I am exaggerating and it won't the first time you try it but that is what happens in the hands of an expert, and the only way to become an expert is to get some tuition and then practice, practice, practice.

There is no doubt that it will pay any salmon fisher to master these casting methods. Their advantages are that they enable you to fish

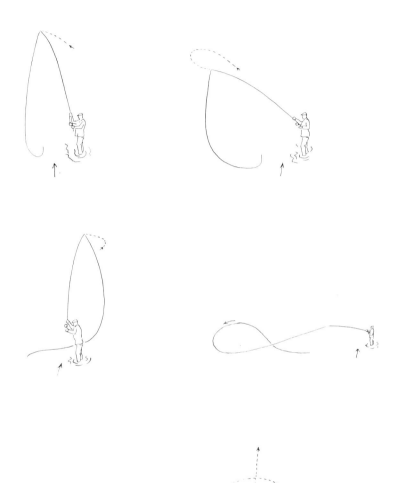

Path of tip of rod as seen from above

Double Spey cast

any closed in part of a river because your fly never passes behind you, they enable you to fish in a very strong downstream wind, and a very strong downstream wind is a real nuisance, far more of a nuisance than a very strong upstream wind, and in the hands of an expert they enable you to cast a very long line indeed. The disadvantages are that they do create more disturbance on the water than the normal over-head cast, they don't really work in a head wind because they haven't the impetus to penetrate it, and it does take time to master them. Also it is difficult to Spey cast properly with rods which have metal ferrules, you need a rod, ideally an old Greenheart, which is spliced and has a continuous action, although I have seen modern carbon fibre rods used very effectively in this way.

There are various other ways to defeat the downstream wind. The main difficulty of a downstream wind is that if you are fishing normally over the correct shoulder, such a wind prevents your line straightening out behind you, it makes it difficult to time your cast properly and you can often end up with your fly hitting you in the back. Apart from the Spey cast and its variations, I know many anglers who simply fish backhanded or over the wrong shoulder. There is no doubt that if there are no obstructions behind you to prevent you doing this then this is a perfectly satisfactory way of proceeding. Some people think that the forward cast is more difficult to time properly if you do this and the fly tends to land rather untidily but many anglers do this most effectively. This is a useful method to teach nervous people who are literally petrified of being caught by their own fly. They seem to gain confidence as the fly cast in this manner is thrown away from their face.

My own preference is to use what is generally known as the 'horse-shoe' cast. Using the handgrip for a right or left shoulder cast you take the fly out over the wrong shoulder and then keep your rod moving round your head in the shape of a horseshoe and bring the line back over the correct shoulder. As your fly is travelling all the time it does not have to straighten out behind you and it is a most effective way to overcome many difficulties. It also produces a very neat end result.

Casting into a head wind, especially if it is of any force, often causes problems to the inexperienced angler and even some experienced fishermen view a head wind with horror. This is quite unnecessary. A head wind, unless it is of absolutely gale force proportions, can really only help you and there is a definite technique to defeating the wind. Having said that there is no doubt that the old-fashioned rods and in

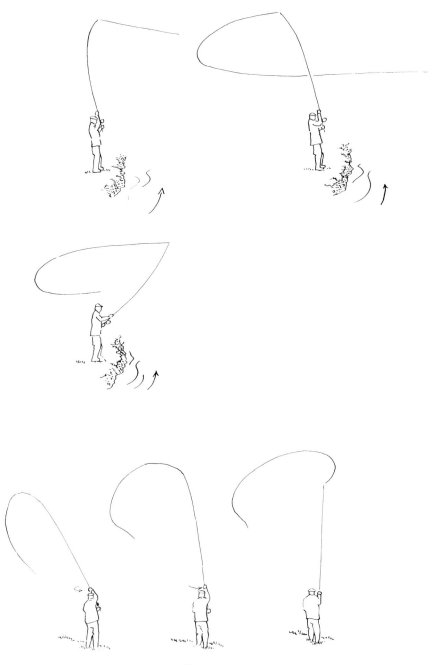

Horseshoe cast

28

particular the old Kingfisher line did cut through a strong wind far more easily than their modern plastic counterparts, but no matter. First of all a head wind will blow your line out behind you and make the timing of your cast much easier. Slow down your timing, then, to get your line to cut through the wind, push your rod down slowly but with rather more controlled force than you would normally employ. Follow through slightly further, pushing the tip of the rod closer to the water than normal and if you are shooting line delay fractionally the moment at which you release the line. Don't whatever you do try to defeat the wind with any sort of what I might call forearm punch allied to any sort of body action. If you do all that will happen is that the fly will shoot forward, lose impetus as soon as it hits the wind and either collapse in a heap or get blown severely off course. Just use your wrists to ease your fly through the wind and again with practice you will be surprised how easily you can cast through quite a strong wind. If there is a side wind then you will have to aim off so to speak, to secure accuracy and also you do on occasions have to beware that the wind may be much stronger out in the river than where you are standing on the bank.

One of the best methods to use if you are dealing with a very strong upstream wind is to back your water up instead of fishing downstream in the normal manner, and in these conditions one of the advantages of backing up your water is that you don't have to cast so accurately.

There is just one more casting variation which is worth knowing about which is a help if you have a high bank behind you. It is called the 'steeple' cast. You use the correct handgrip but position your hands wider apart than normal and then you really just lift your rod more vertically than normal when you come to cast. This will throw your line high in the air above you but it can be difficult to time your forward cast correctly, particularly if awkward conditions prevail. This or the technique of reversing your handgrip on the rod to prevent it going too far back, a technique I have seen used by some anglers, can give you up to 15 feet increased lift on your back cast, but personally I would Spey cast if I could, rather than be constantly worried whether I was lifting my fly high enough out of the water.

Some anglers, probably particularly trout anglers, who have been used to casting round obstacles on small trout streams, can improvise casts to enable them to surmount awkward physical obstructions or undergrowth encroaching into a pool. Indeed there was one particular ghillie on the Naver, now gathered to his fathers, who could literally

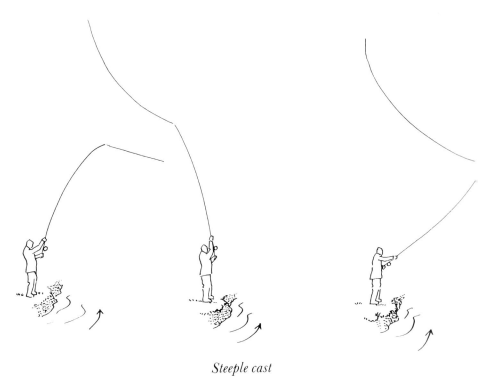

Steeple cast

cast directly upstream and angle his fly precisely as he wished. I have never seen anyone else who had quite this skill but if you are attempting trick casts of this nature you must direct your rod with your wrists.

There is no doubt, and it is the same with every game or sport, that if you learn to cast properly at an early age then you have a tremendous advantage. I have noticed that fishermen who learnt as young boys nearly all use their wrists properly and keep their bodies straight when they cast, which are the two worst faults commonly found in the inexperienced.

There is one final point which I might have made in the chapter *Fishing a Pool* but I will make here. Certain pools have a strong backwater on the same side as the angler is fishing from, and if you are not careful then this will drown your line between the fly and the rod tip. If you are fishing a pool which has this type of backwater then you should hold your rod higher and keep contact with your fly the whole time as it traverses the pool and make absolutely certain that your fly is buoyant before you cast again. If you are in doubt switch your fly out of the water downstream before lifting it off to make your next cast. If you do not take these precautions it is highly likely that you may strain your rod badly or even worse break the centre joint when you attempt to cast.

In some pools which have two streams entering at the head there is every chance of a backwater current in between these two streams, and if you do not watch out and handline quickly then your line may become trapped in this backwater and be driven upstream towards you in which case you may make an expensive mistake. The classic example of a pool of this type is the Round Pool on the Lower Cassley, especially when the pool is fished from the left bank. I have heard this pool spoken of, even by experienced fishermen as a horrible pool which is a grave-yard for rods. I cannot resist quoting to them the passage from Lord Grey's *Fly Fishing* which gives the most beautiful description of this pool and how it should be fished.

'Below the rough water comes the Round Pool – a deep basin with rock bottom. The water enters in two streams, one slanting to the left and the other running close along the right bank. When the water is low the angler must fish each of these streams separately, and there is always a chance, even in very low water, that a fish may come in either of them. In high water the two streams unite: there is slack water between them and the left bank, and the main outflow is a deep smooth glide to the left bottom corner. From its smoothness, in contrast with the turbulent upper part of the stream, we called this "the glass"; and when the pool first became fishable after a spate in April, this spot was the greatest certainty (as far as anything in fishing can be certain) for getting a salmon that I have known on the Cassley or on any river. Owing to the set of the current this spot, when in order, can be fished effectively only from the right bank, and at the head of the pool Providence has placed a large stone, large enough indeed to be dignified with the name of Rock. It is smooth, very little above the level of the water, with ample room behind for overhead casting, and with a depression in the top of it which led to our calling it the "cup stone". In this an angler can stand and thence command the whole pool, and finally, by raising the point of the rod, can hang the fly most attractively in "the glass". There is still another expedient to be tried. At a last resort the longest possible cast should be made to the bottom left-hand corner, and the line reeled up as slowly as the angler has patience to do it. In any choice spot this method often succeeds when all else has failed. When a fish has been hooked, the angler can step back on to the low bank, which is flush with the top of the cup stone, move down to the bottom of the pool, play the fish from this advantageous position, and finally draw it onto a bed of shingle which has been formed by a small burn that comes in immediately below the pool. If I were asked to name a place where Nature had, as if by design, done everything possible to please or help a salmon angler, I should say without doubt the Round Pool on the Cassley.'

Fishing a Pool

On every river there are two very different types of pool. First the large holding pool which is inhabited by resident fish at all heights of water and secondly the smaller run or resting pool which holds fish only at certain heights of water, when they are running or when a very high river makes them change their lies. If you are lucky enough to find fish that have just entered one of these pools then very often they can be more productive than the genuine holding pools because there is no doubt that the longer a fish stays in one pool the more difficult they become to catch. It is always the fish that is on the move, either changing lies in the pool or moving upstream that is the most likely to be caught provided he is settled in the lie.

If you go to a pool for the first time it will pay you to examine it for a minute or two before rushing to fish it straight away, to assess whether there are any obvious lies visible on the surface. A swirl in the water shows some of these lies because these are caused by underwater rocks which break the force of the current. Salmon will lie both in front and behind these rocks, because there they are protected from the main force of the current. When you fish a pool for the first time it is well worth paying particular attention to these places.

In any pool there are two places where fish can normally be taken. At the head where fish will lie on either side of the deep stream entering the pool. Over the years such streams will have washed away the particles of sand and gravel leaving large rocks which give ideal shelter to the fish resident in the pool and at the tail where there is often quieter water covering large boulders as the current quickens towards the draw at the exit of the pool. Particularly when fish are running or in high water fish rest behind these boulders after ascending the rapids which lie below most pools. And any pool that has a long

Taking places

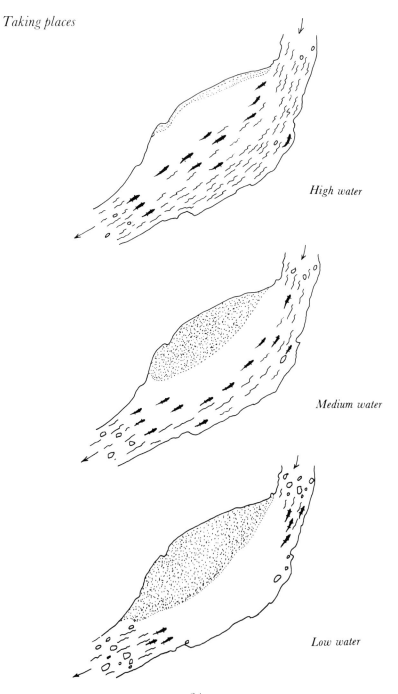

High water

Medium water

Low water

length of rapids below it is almost certain to hold fish in the tail.

Until you get to know a pool intimately then, certainly you will get the best results by covering every inch of the pool thoroughly. The best taking places in any pool will vary tremendously according to the height of the water. So if you are successful in one place at one height of water do not be surprised if you catch fish in quite a different place at a different height of water. Fish may still be lying where you first caught them but because the set of the current has altered your fly may not fish the lie properly, for even 2 or 3 inches more or less of water in a pool can alter the position of the taking lies drastically.

In high water fish lie on the edge of the fast currents, in the main body of the pool where the current is less strong and probably the best place of all is at the tail of the pool, very often right on the lip of the draw where fish will rest when they are running. In medium water most pools will fish the whole way down and you should fish each pool right out carefully unless you have a ghillie or companion with you who knows from experience that certain parts of the pool are not worth fishing at that height of water. In low water pay particular attention to the neck of the pool, particularly if it is streamy and fish it down as far as the current allows you to work your fly properly. Also fish the tail if it has a draw and of course if there is any wind ruffling the surface the whole pool can be backed up.

When you start to fish a pool always take the length of the line on the rod and make your first cast with this, work it quietly with your rod tip so that you fish the water right in to where you are standing and then strip off a yard of line and do the same thing again. Continue pulling off a yard of line at a time and fishing it out thoroughly until you have sufficient line out to cover the far side of the current. Only then do you start moving down the pool. I call this 'fanning out your line' and if you do not do this you can miss fish that are lying close to you right in the head of the pool. I have known many anglers, even experienced ones, fail to do this properly merely lengthening their line until it is landing on the far side of the pool and thereby they miss many fish who are lying close in within the arc between the angler and where the fly lands and this is a mistake which undoubtedly saves many fishes' lives.

When you pull out your line work the fly with the rod tip only for the first few casts and only begin to handline when you have cast out a sufficient length of line that your rod can throw in comfort. If you handline too soon you leave too short a length of line on the rod to lead out what is in your hand; then you will have to false cast to shoot out this line and that is both bad for your rod and also can frighten any fish lying close to you. Fish are definitely frightened by any quick rod movement and I have often seen fish frightened out of their lies by an angler false casting. If you do have to false cast do it with a roll of your wrists right close in to your bank without lifting your rod over your shoulder and that way you will keep such disturbance to a minimum.

Once you have enough line out to cover the width of the pool or the fishable water then move down the pool approximately a yard per cast. Never move while your fly is actually fishing. Wait till your fly has come right across the fishable water and is directly below you and then move down as you handline to make your fly buoyant before casting again. If you do move down when your fly is fishing across the pool you are not in a position to strike or tighten if a fish takes you and also inevitably your fly will back down the current which makes it less attractive to the fish.

Especially in high water conditions it is very important to work your fly right into the bank as this is often a favourite taking place. As your fly crosses the pool you should lead your fly into the bank and then work the point of the rod outwards again so that when the fly comes into the bank your rod tip is almost square to the current. By doing this you will get a better angle of strike on any fish taking close into the bank immediately below you.

Always keep a careful eye on your fly as it crosses the pool. Very often you will see a swirl in the water or even a head and tail rise as a fish moves to your fly. Unless you feel the fish it is important that you do nothing when this happens. Let your fly fish out the cast and then move back three or four yards and come down over the fish again. If he does not come to you at the second attempt, make a mark in the ground with your heel or take a bearing so that you know his exact position so that you can try him later and then fish out the rest of the pool. Many anglers keep casting over a fish they have moved. This can work on occasions but I think it best to move back three or four yards to give the fish a moment's rest and allow it time to return to its lie before trying it again.

Many, many times I have seen anglers lessen their chances of success by the way they approach their water. Generally, especially in high water or in the spring, the cautious approach of the chalk stream fisherman after trout, is not strictly speaking necessary, but in summer and when water levels are low, there is no doubt that a careless approach to the water can be harmful. If a salmon is frightened then it will drop back into the still deep parts of the pool and when it has done this it is very difficult to catch indeed. Salmon are far easier to catch on a fly when they are undisturbed in fairly shallow water or lying at a reasonable depth in the deeper pools. Therefore it is a mistake to walk up the river bank close to the water's edge, particularly if there is a fairly high bank, when with a little thought one can walk up the bank 10 or 15 yards from the water. Also, particularly in the summer, it is a mistake to approach right to the water's edge when fishing the head of a pool when the water can be just as easily covered standing four or five yards above and away from the pool.

Similarly if you have someone with you don't let them stand opposite where your fly is working. Make them stand beside you or sit at a distance where they can do no harm. Another point to watch is the behaviour of dogs. I am not against dogs accompanying their masters to the river bank. Far from it. They are not only good company but provided they behave well do no harm at all but the patter of dogs' feet on a solid surface, and its quick actions, are almost identical to those of an otter. Often when I have been fishing a gorgy pool, standing well above the fish, I have seen them disappear when my sister's dog rushed up to me. So if you do have your dog with you keep it away from the bank as much as you can, particularly if you are fishing a beat with a number of rocky ledges which transmit the vibration.

Any vibrations can have a disastrous effect on fish lying in a pool. There is a pool on the Welsh Dee below Llangollen called the Pentre Pool, heavily wooded on the right bank, which has a rock ledge running down the length of the pool. At fishable heights of water this ledge is about 18 inches under water and the pool can easily be fished by any angler wading down the ledge. In twenty years' experience of this pool I have known the occasional fish taken from the pool fished in this way and I mean occasional. However if the pool was fished from a coracle with the handler quietly holding the coracle in position over the ledge, exactly where the angler waded down, then many fish could be taken from the pool and indeed at good heights of water it was one of the most productive on our beat. On several occasions to satisfy myself that it was the vibration caused by wading down the ledge that put the fish off, I fished the pool from the ledge first, inevitably with no result, and then I fished the pool from the coracle with the same fly and very often I was successful. I have known rocky pools bordering arable land, that normally were very productive, produce no fish when a tractor was working in the neighbouring fields, and I always put this down to the vibration transmitted through the rock outcrops disturbing the fish.

Bearing this in mind I think that all anglers should be careful when they start wading down a pool. Many times, of course, it is necessary to wade and there are many pools which cannot be fished properly without wading. But I have seen anglers using breast waders heading in far too deep, often in a direct line with where fish are lying and this will inevitably disturb them. If you know a pool well or you have the benefit of guidance from a ghillie then this is unlikely to happen, but if you are in doubt then it is best to err on the side of safety and wade as close to your bank as you can, assuming that you can cover the pool properly. Sometimes you can find an obvious bank of gravel that you can wade down without causing disturbance, but you should also be careful not to let the water from your waders flow directly over the lies in the pool you are fishing. Many fishermen I know say that they have caught fish directly downstream of the point where they were wading. This may be perfectly correct but it depends very much on the set of the current, the flow of water in the river and the dilution rate that prevails. Remember that all salmon have a very acute sense of smell and experiments have shown that salmon ascending a fish pass or jumping a falls can be stopped if a human hand is immersed in the water above the falls, even though the person was out of sight of the fish.

Backing up a Pool

Backing up a pool means precisely what it says. Instead of starting at the top of the pool and fishing it down to the bottom as normal you start at the bottom of the pool and work your way up to the head of it. Many fishermen do not know of this way of fishing and many more despise it but it is a most effective method of fishing which can not only often save a blank day, but often account for a very large proportion of the fish killed on a good one. It has many advantages over the authentic method. First of all you can back up many pools which have insufficient current to work the fly properly and it will enable you to fish completely dead water perfectly satisfactorily, provided there is sufficient wind to ruffle the surface. Secondly if there is a very strong upstream wind, so strong that it makes normal downstream fishing virtually impossible, then backing up a pool will enable you to cheat the wind very effectively. Thirdly because when you are backing up a pool you are moving upstream and are therefore in direct touch with your fly, the proportion of hooked fish that are landed is much higher than it is for the authentic downstream method and fourthly it enables you to fish a pool in a much shorter time than the authentic method.

Backing up a pool presents the fly in an entirely different way to the fish. The first sight the fish has of the fly is when it appears from behind him and I think that it is this reason that makes it so effective. I think possibly the salmon views the fly as a fish trying to escape and is prompted to cut it off.

If you are going to back up a pool then you should keep away from the water's edge and walk down to the tail. Cast out your line until it is landing on the far side of the fishable water and you do not have to fan your fly out with care as you do when starting at the head of the pool. Also cast rather squarer across the current than you would normally and as soon as you have got sufficient line out, start handlining in slowly and at the same time move three or four steady paces upstream towards the head of the pool. You are best to move three or four paces each cast and adjust the speed that you handline to the speed of the current, and as you watch your fly come across the stream it will be obvious how fast or slowly you should do this. If there is a very strong upstream wind you can cast square across the pool or even slightly upstream because you can adjust the speed you move up the bank and the speed that you handline to take account of this. When you reach the head of the pool you must finish the pool off properly as otherwise you will fail to cover what can be a very productive bit of water. Stand still in the same place and then wind in a yard or two each cast until you only have the length of line on the rod left. Only if you do this will you finish off the pool correctly. I have many times seen even experienced anglers make this mistake just reeling up when they have got to the head of the pool and as a result they miss any fish lying in the top 15 yards of the pool.

Many fishermen, particularly those getting on in years, are frightened of backing their way up uneven river banks. In fact it is generally a good deal easier than you might think and on many rivers and pools there is a beaten path which runs up the pool three or four yards from the water's edge. It is much better to use this path if one exists than try to stumble over rough ground because generally when backing up, because you are casting squarer across the current you do not have to cast so far so the sacrifice of distance is of little importance. If you do have to fish a pool which has a very uneven bank with no path then you are better to turn your back on your fly and walk upstream, handlining at the same time. It won't affect the presentation of your fly and if a fish takes you then, because you are in direct contact with the fly, you will feel the fish and be able to strike directly. If you have to turn your back on the water try and keep glancing over your shoulder as you walk upstream because then you are more likely to see the boil if a fish moves to your fly. If this happens go three or four yards down the bank and try the fish again but if you don't get a take on the second occasion mark the spot on the bank before fishing out the rest of the pool and you can then cover that fish with particular care when you fish the pool again with another fly. Of course if you have a ghillie with you, he will warn you if you have risen a fish when your back is turned and you can take the appropriate action.

It is possible to back up a pool that requires wading but unless the

Backing up a Pool

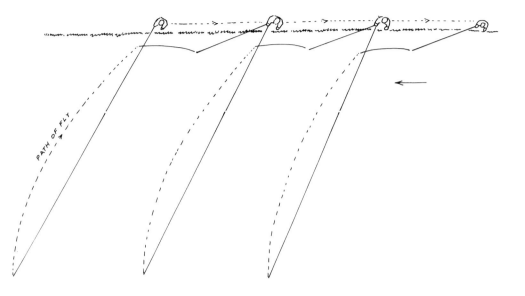

Backing up a pool

bottom is very smooth you do have to be very careful and feel your way upstream with care. As a general tip when wading never lift your feet too high and always make sure that one foot is firmly anchored before you move the next one. This applies particularly when wading upstream against the current and here a wading stick really isn't the help it can be when wading downstream.

If the bottom is very uneven but you really do want to back up the pool then it is probably best to cast out and then turn your back on the fly and work your way two or three steps upstream. When you have reached the point from where you want to make your next cast fish the remainder of the cast out by handlining. This method can be quite effective but naturally enough it does not impart quite the same flowing movement to the fly as the proper method. But, and I stress this, it does enable you to fish pools and dead water that would be quite unfishable in any other way.

If you are fishing dead water, or a pool which has insufficient current to enable your fly to work across the width of the pool, then backing up is much the most effective way to overcome these difficulties. In these conditions it is the movement of the angler up the bank dragging the fly behind him, that gives the fly impetus to

41

traverse the width of the pool and the act of handlining only assists this process. If you try to fish this type of water by handlining alone you will find it not only extremely laborious but also the amount of line you have to pull in to fish the fly properly right into the bank will usually be far more than you can shoot when you re-cast. This necessitates false casting which is a thing to be avoided.

Don't forget that there are two times of the year when you are likely to find a large proportion of the fish in the river lying in this type of water. The first is in the early spring when water temperatures are very low when the fish like to lie out of the main force of the current. The second is in high summer because then the fish can lie deep unaffected by the scorching rays of the sun, in lies that are normally very well oxygenated at these temperatures.

The only essential ingredient necessary to fish this type of pool is wind, which must be strong enough to ruffle the water where the fish are lying. An upstream wind inevitably is the best because relatively it produces a bigger wave per gust velocity and the bigger the wave the better such a pool will fish. A six-inch wave is as good as a six-inch rise in the water and, particularly in the summer after an hour or two of a good wind, you will often see all the fish in a pool start to show themselves and porpoise about on the top of the water. Under these conditions you are very likely to be successful, because long pools will now fish from head to tail when, without a wind only the top fifteen or twenty yards would have sufficient current to be fished properly, and on these long pools backing up is the ideal method to fish the entire length of the pool and cover fish that may not have seen a fly for several days if the weather has been calm.

Backing up is also a good way to teach the novice or the inexperienced fisherman the timing of the strike. One of the commonest faults is for the beginner, particularly if he has come to salmon fishing from trout fishing, to strike too soon as he sees the rise of the fish to the fly. This means that they inevitably pull the fly away from the fish. It is essential to wait until you feel the fish before striking and if you are in charge of a novice who has this fault, make him or her back the pool up with their back to their fly. Then if a fish takes they will feel the pull first and I have found this an effective way of overcoming this fault.

Many people ask me what flies I use when backing up. This does depend on why you are backing up a pool and normally I use exactly the same fly as I would if I was fishing the pool in the authentic manner. Thus if I was backing up a pool because there was insufficient current to fish it properly, or because there was a very strong upstream wind, or because the pool was so long that I wanted to cover it quickly or because I wanted to circumvent an awkward backwater on my side of the current, then I would always use a normal size of fly. Then if I wanted to back the pool up for a second time I would put on a bigger fly assuming that the first fly had been unsuccessful.

If however I was backing a pool up because all else had failed then I would generally put on a much bigger fly, probably one of the long-tailed hair tube flies, and fish it slightly faster to try to entice the lethargic fish into action. Don't forget that while backing up was invented to enable the angler to cover difficult and dead water, it can be equally effective in pools which have a good current through them. If I am fishing a holding pool in springtime I always fish it down first in the normal way and then back it up without even winding in my fly. I often move or catch several fish on the way back up the pool which I was not aware of moving on the way down. Maybe some of these had moved to the fly without breaking the surface but I am sure some are enticed by the different presentation.

Regardless of the height of water in the springtime I never give up until I have backed up a pool using a Collie Dog six inches or larger. Very often I have found that this type of shock tactic will move a number of fish and on occasions you will kill the fish that saves the blank by using this method. And in the summer I do the same with a Collie Dog, two inches in length. If you do move a fish to a ridiculously large fly using this method it is then worth backing up the pool again using a normal size of fly and very often the fish that has moved to the larger fly will take the smaller one solidly. Maybe the sight of the large fly wakes them from a trance, I don't know, but the number of times I have been successful using these tactics proves to me that it is no fluke. And I will go further and say that if you move nothing to a very large Collie Dog fished like this then you are most unlikely to be successful with anything else.

But a word of warning, don't use these tactics except as a last resort, because if you do then you are likely to prick a number of fish that might have taken a small fly solidly. If you find when you are backing up a pool that you are moving a number of fish without touching them, it may well be that you are fishing your fly too fast or too slowly. It is well worth varying the speed of your presentation which may make absolutely no difference to the result but is certainly worth trying. On my beat of the Cassley and on many other beats in adjoining rivers, particularly in the springtime, it would be quite true to say that fifty per cent or more of the fish killed are killed backing up and if more anglers adopted this method of presentation throughout the country it would increase the total number of salmon killed on the fly quite appreciably.

To Strike or not to Strike

This is probably the most controversial subject in all salmon fishing and there is no doubt in my mind that it is what the angler chooses to do at the point of contact that is responsible in many cases for a fish being merely pricked, hooked and lost, or landed.

There are three schools of thought. The first school of thought, of which I am a firm adherent, says you must raise your rod point firmly and instantaneously, in other words, strike immediately you feel the fish. The second school of thought says you should merely raise your rod point and let the weight of the fish and the strength of the current drive the hook in. The third school of thought says you must have a loop of line which you should let the fish pull out of your hand before tightening. The logic behind this school of thought is that it allows time for the fly in the fish's mouth to turn and be drawn into the hinge so that the fish is invariably well hooked.

There are two things that any fisherman must consider when deciding what to do. The first is the shape and design of a salmon's mouth, and the second is the various ways that a salmon takes a fly. Dealing first with a salmon's mouth. This is really 'V' shaped. The top and bottom of the 'V' are the jawbones which are very hard and are covered by a thin, but tough film of skin. The soft parts of the mouth are the tongue, the roof of the mouth, the muscle behind the 'hinge' at the corner of the mouth, and the gullet which is very soft. If you are going to stand any chance of landing a salmon then you have to drive your hook in over the barb. This is fairly easily achieved in the soft parts of the mouth, but obviously more power is required to penetrate the armoured areas. Also the distance between the point of the hook and the barb does necessarily vary enormously according to the size of the fly you are using or will use during the course of the season.

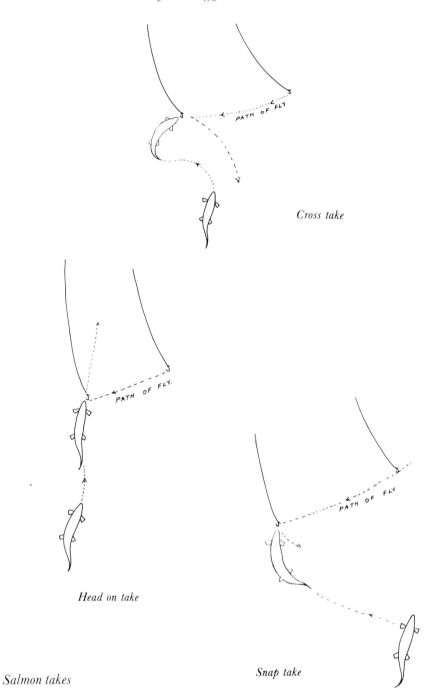

Cross take

Head on take

Snap take

Salmon takes

The next thing to consider is the various ways in which a salmon takes a fly. These vary over the season, and it is therefore of vital importance to bear this in mind when you tighten or strike, and you must learn to gauge the power with which you strike correctly. I have had the good fortune to fish for many years on a river which allows me to observe from a height salmon taking a fly, and I have learnt more from this than I could have done in any other way. I therefore know for a fact that there are three main ways in which a salmon takes a fly. The first of these is what I call the good boy who really hooks himself. As the fly comes across the stream the salmon comes out from its lie, cuts in between the bank which the fly is moving towards and the fly itself and takes it as he moves back towards the centre of the river angling downstream slightly as he does so in order to return to his lie. I call this the crosstake and if a fish takes in this way then he will generally be well hooked whether you strike, do nothing, or let a loop of line run out.

The second sort of take is the fish that comes straight up at the fly, and takes it literally head on. This type of fish quite often moves a considerable distance upstream with the fly in his mouth, before moving back into the depths and turning back to his lie. Therefore if a fish takes in this way while, if the angler is fishing with a greased line he may, indeed usually will, see the fish move to the fly, while if he is fishing with a sunk fly he may not, and the only thing he may notice is a hesitation in his line and feel a faint brush as the fish takes the fly into its mouth. Now it is very important to make absolutely clear what I mean by instantaneous strike. I don't mean that you should strike like the trout fishermen when you see the movement of the fish, but when you feel the fish make contact with the fly. If you have a fish which takes you head-on and carries the fly upstream and you do not see any movement on the surface I strike immediately I feel the faint brush. If however I see the fish move to the fly I count very firmly 1, 2, 3 and then I strike. It is rather like striking the largest chalk stream trout you ever caught where in the words of J. W. Hills, 'You must give these gentlemen plenty of time.'

Now consider in this instance what happens to the other two schools of thought, and consider what the fish does when it comes upstream with what can only be described as a hard piece of ironmongery in its mouth. These fish may or may not be moving very fast and particularly in the summer they are quite often moving fairly slowly. Just occasionally you will meet one so obliging that it continues to hold the fly in its mouth and eventually it turns downstream to return to its lie. In this case all is well whatever you do and the fish will be hooked. More usually, however, and I have seen this time and time again, the fish ejects the fly immediately it has closed its mouth on it. Fish which do this give a quick shake of their head and literally spit the fly out in a shower of bubbles. Therefore unless you strike, either having counted three after you have seen the fish head and tail to the fly, or immediately if you feel a faint brush and see the line hesitate in the water then you won't hook a salmon that takes you in this way. If you strike you will generally find that fish who take like this are hooked at the back of the tongue which is where the salmon holds the fly just before he ejects it.

I have proved this to myself time and time again but one story will illustrate what I mean. One afternoon I walked down to the Cassley where my late father was fishing. He told me that he had moved a large fish to a small Black Doctor five times but hadn't touched it. I asked him if he had struck the fish and he said he hadn't. He then told me to have a go so I took his rod and the fish made a head and tail rise to the same fly. Having allowed the fish to submerge I struck and hooked the fish firmly in the back of its tongue. It was probable that this fish had taken the fly five times in a head and tail manner and ejected it five times, and this can happen far more often than many anglers realise.

The third and last type of take, is one which occurs most often when a fly is being fished deep or in unsettled water conditions when fish come up behind the fly or less often across it and just literally snap at it, opening their mouths almost as soon as they have closed them. Many experienced anglers call this coming short. But when you consider this you should also consider the number of fish that move to a fly and even in low water conditions, leave no visible blemish on the surface of the water. Many of these fish have no intention of taking the fly. Some come no closer to the fly than two feet while others will come within a fraction of an inch of the fly, and it is only when you have a vantage point over a pool that you can see this. Now if a fish behaves like this and just snaps at the fly the only chance that you have of hooking it is if you strike, and strike quickly, though I don't pretend it is a very good one. Otherwise you will just feel the tug and that will be all.

Before I finish I would say that there are two other occasions when you definitely should not strike, and I will explain why. If you are dibbling in the summer you must, as I say in my chapter on *Summer Fishing*, give the fish time to take the fly down and if you strike immediately you will pull the fly away from the fish. The second occasion is if you are fishing with floating line and, like Wood imitating plankton, hanging in the current. If you are doing this properly then you will not be in direct contact with your fly, you are therefore not in a position to strike immediately and you are well advised to count slowly to three before tightening.

On most occasions, and it is well for every salmon fisherman to bear this in mind, the boil that he sees at the fly is made by the tail of the fish as it turns away from the fly, and *not* by the movement of the fish towards the fly. If I see a boil at my fly, and this is particularly true if I am backing up a pool or fishing any type of dead water, then I always count to three and then strike for it may be that the fish has come forward to the fly and is carrying it down in its mouth. If that is the case then I will hook the fish before it can eject the fly and if it is not the case then the fish has turned far enough away for it not to be disturbed by the strike.

I think there is another point which should be borne in mind by all fishermen. One of the main reasons for allowing the fish time before striking was supposedly to allow the fly time to slide into the hinge of the mouth. This was all very well when fishermen used single hooked flies exclusively, and it is even a reasonable supposition with double hooked flies. Nowadays, however, the vast majority of fishermen use trebles of various sizes or Edmund Drury flies and personally I very much doubt whether it is possible for a salmon to close his mouth on a hook of this type without one of the points penetrating some part of it which will prevent the hook sliding in the mouth, and therefore the fish will be hooked in the part of the mouth where the hook is first lodged. I would also say that I have struck all the salmon I have caught for many, many years and I hook a large proportion of them in the hinge or scissors so I really do doubt whether the loose line is necessary in the first place.

Finally I must add a word or two of warning. The purpose of striking when a salmon takes you is to drive the hook into its mouth over the barb, the force necessary to do this will vary with the length of line you are casting, the type of rod you are using, if it is stiff or supple, and the size of fly. Timing, confidence and technique are all important but if you wish to test the necessity and it is a very simple way to experiment, go out with a friend with a salmon rod and hold onto the fly in your hand. If your friend quietly tightens the line by raising the rod gently you will find you can open your hand and let the fly go or at the very worst the point will just penetrate the skin. I know for I have done it. However a quick pull will produce quite a different story and a painful visit to the doctor. On this I rest my case.

Playing a Fish

When you have hooked a salmon, the next stage is to play and hopefully land your fish. Every angler knows those heartbreaking sequences when nearly every fish hooked seems to drop off and there is no one who can guarantee to land every fish he hooks but in my opinion it is possible to minimise the number of losses that occur, and this can be done by taking the correct action once the fish is hooked.

First of all, as I have stated in the chapter on *Striking*, it is most important to set the hook firmly in the salmon's mouth so that the hook penetrates over the barb. If only the point is embedded then the hook can quickly be thrown either by a shake of the fish's head or a moment of slack line. The force necessary to set the hook properly does, of course, vary with the size and type of fly you are using and if you are using a large old-fashioned single hooked fly where the distance from the point of the hook to the end of the barb may be as much as ¼ inch, then you will have to strike much more firmly than with a size 10 low water fly. The force you will have to use also varies with the length and power of your rod. The larger the rod the less force is necessary and you will have to learn this by experience.

However if I can assume that you have set your hook firmly in the fish's mouth, you then have no reason to hold the fish tightly immediately this has been done. Indeed to do so is a mistake. The hook will not fall out and if you want to test this drive a hook into your hand – but I don't advise it.

At the moment of contact the fish receives a severe fright and is therefore inclined to panic. The more tightly you hold a fish the more fiercely it will fight, and I have seen beginners clinging on to the line while the salmon remains thrashing on the surface of the water. This generally results in a broken cast or the hookhold tearing away. So

once the fish has been hooked make sure you keep your rod up and
apply even pressure, then let the fish submerge and run and do exactly
what it wants for the first few minutes and provided you have a sweet
running reel then this will be no problem.

If you are fishing from the bank the next thing you have to do is to
walk down to get level with your fish but if you are wading then you
must come ashore. Don't rush this. If you are wading deeply in
difficult conditions then trying to come ashore too quickly can result in
a fall which can jerk the hook from its hold. It is far better to forget
about the fish and work your way steadily to the bank, and I even
know anglers whose practice it is to turn their backs to the river and
wade ashore with the rod held over their shoulders. If the hook has
been set properly then it won't fall out. Once you have reached the
bank then you can reel in and re-establish contact with the fish.

It is important to keep the point of your rod well up and hold the
butt into your midriff with your left hand, assuming that you are
right-handed, and keep the forefinger of your left hand on the line. If
you do this you will get a far better warning of what the fish is going to
do than if you attempt to play it just off the reel and this is particularly
important towards the end of the fight when the battle is almost won
and the fish is on the surface. If an exhausted fish gets broadside on in
a strong current the force of the current is quite sufficient to make the
reel run out freely which can needlessly lengthen the time it takes to
play your salmon. By increasing the pressure of your forefinger you
can prevent this and at the same time you can judge the remaining
strength of the fish much better than if you relied on the tension on the
reel alone. One word of warning, at the beginning of the fight, if the
fish makes a long run at speed you should not touch the line at all, for
if you do you can get a nasty friction burn.

I have often seen anglers place their hands on the drum of the reel
or even hold on to the reel handle. Either of these methods is foolish in
the extreme. At the best if the fish makes a sudden run it can mean a
nasty rap on the knuckles, at worst it will wrench the fly from the fish's
mouth or break the cast. Also do keep the rod point held high. If you
do this it will act as a spring which will absorb the shock of any sudden
movement on the part of the fish and it also wears down the fish's
strength. This is one of the commonest faults of the beginner to salmon
fishing. If you let the point of the rod drop and the line is straight then
there is only the elasticity of the cast and the line itself left to absorb
any sudden actions, on the part of the salmon, such as an unexpected

jump, and this may well result in a broken cast or a torn hookhold.

As soon as possible after hooking your salmon get level with it and keep it on as short a line as possible. If you play a fish on too long a line then there is every chance that your line will get drowned which increases the pressure on the hookhold or even worse allows the line to get snagged. If your fish tries to get above you move upstream and try to get level with him.

A number of people like to try and make their fish swim upstream, reasoning that if you make the salmon contend with the force of the current then it will get tired more quickly. I am not certain that this is in fact correct for fish find it easier to breathe in fast flowing water and you can definitely kill fish more quickly in slack water. Also if a fish gets a long way upstream of you, you are generally reversing the angle of your original hookhold, and if either the stale of an ordinary fly, or one or two hooks of a treble catch against its jawbone, they can act as a lever and pull the hook out of the fish's mouth in exactly the same way as you extract the fly from the salmon's mouth when you have landed it. Another disadvantage is if the fish makes a sudden turn downstream the current can often draw your sunk line round a rock, often in such a way that you cannot free it, with disastrous results. If a fish is a long way below you and then turns upstream then there is not the same danger because the current will help to keep your line free from snags, and even if it does get snagged can often easily be released. If you can keep roughly level with your fish then either of these dangers can be avoided.

Always try and keep your fish in the pool where it was hooked. This isn't always possible and particularly when you are young it can be most exhilarating to charge down the bank with the reel screaming but I don't advise it if you can avoid it. If you hook a fish near the tail of a pool and it threatens to go down out of the pool then you can very often stop it by dropping the point of your rod and even pulling off some line. When the fish ceases to feel any pressure then say eight times out of ten it will turn round and start to swim back to its lie. Once you have the fish quiet then you can walk it up away from danger. If however you keep holding on to your fish and you cannot follow it down then you have no alternative but to hang on for grim death which will mean almost inevitably a torn hookhold or a broken cast or line which is worse.

People often ask me how you walk up a salmon and whether it works. The answer is yes, it works very easily and there is no difficulty about it at all. Keep a steady even pressure on the fish and then start to walk slowly up the bank, and the fish will follow you upstream like a well-trained dog. Don't however touch your reel. If you do the vibrations will run down the line and start the fish pulling away from you again. Once you have walked the fish up to a position of safety in the pool, you can increase the pressure and start reeling in to make the fish run again.

Once you have settled your fish down gradually increase the pressure and it will soon begin to tire. I don't personally believe that fish should be killed within a certain time as the length of time you take to play a fish will depend most of all on the fish, but also the pool, the strength of the current and a number of other factors. However there is definitely the danger of being too soft on a fish and obviously the quicker a fish is killed the less likelihood there is of the hookhold wearing away, but the corollary of this is not to be in any way impatient with a salmon particularly when it begins to tire and come in. It is then that the beginner is most likely to be caught out by a sudden movement on the part of the fish – in particular a sudden and unexpected jump. With experience you will develop a sixth sense of when a salmon will jump, and here I should say that some will jump a good deal while others will not jump at all. Salmon very often jump after a quick lunge in the water or at the end of a long run, it is when a salmon jumps suddenly when it is on a short line that the beginner is most likely to be caught out. When a fish jumps you must drop your rod point immediately and practice this until it becomes quite automatic. For if you do not do this, thereby allowing enough slack line to compensate for the jerk which will follow when the fish re-enters the water, then the jerk will very likely pull the fly out or break a light cast.

So don't be soft on your fish but don't at the same time try and finish the battle prematurely. Again experience will teach you more than all the words ever written, but remember that when they first come into shallow water all salmon will make one last desperate bid for freedom and at this stage it is better to keep up an even tug-of-war rather than try to haul your fish to shore prematurely, which will often make it struggle and thrash the water. Remember that a quick slap on the line by the salmon's tail can often loosen the hookhold and if you put too much strain on you can weaken your cast and strain the temper of your hook. Trebles especially can either snap or straighten out depending on whether they are over or under tempered and the loss of a fish at this stage is particularly aggravating.

Another manoeuvre which often takes the beginner by surprise is when the salmon makes a sudden turn towards you or swims right in under your bank. If the salmon does this then don't initially be too worried by the slack line and don't either handline or reel in too quickly. If you handline then your line may easily snag round a frond of bracken or some of the sweet smelling bog myrtle which so often lines the banks of rivers and if you reel in too quickly without keeping sufficient pressure on your line you can create snags deep down in your reel which can be fatal when the fish takes another run or you next hook a fish that takes out a lot of line. Reel in calmly until you have re-established contact with your fish and if the fish comes right in under your bank, walk backwards until the pull of the fish is no longer directly under the tip of your rod.

The final difficulty that you may meet is playing a fish which sulks and inevitably it is the big fish which do this. A sulking fish is one which dives down to the bottom and stands on its head, so to speak, with its tail up. Fish which do this can remain in this position for an inordinate period of time. I have found that the best way to deal with this is to bring your rod down almost level with the bank and keep a steady side strain on the fish. This is inclined to tilt it off balance and very often has the desired effect and makes it fight. You can try throwing stones into the pool above the fish and I have heard of people trying to throw sand in above the fish on the theory that the grit gets into the gills and the salmon will move away from it. But alas I know of many instances where this has happened and the unseen 'fish of a lifetime' has got free, because a knot has finally slipped or the fly worked loose. The only infallible way of shifting a fish that does this was demonstrated to me by an old ghillie on the Welsh Dee, when I was a boy. I remember a big fish being hooked and after a short while diving down to the bottom and sulking. Nothing would move it. The old ghillie suddenly took hold of the angler's line and taking a piece of rolled Black Twist tobacco from his pocket, he whipped the tobacco in a ring round the line. Then he loosed the line and the ring of tobacco ran down the line and lodged in the vicinity of the hookhold. The salmon quite literally went mad and was landed a short time afterwards. The ghillie explained that he had used this trick many times with success, his theory was that the juice from the tobacco was taken into the fish's gills with very painful effects, I have seen keyrings and lumps of lead used in this way but they don't have the same inevitable result but nowadays, of course, it is rare to have a ghillie who smokes rolled Black Twist!

Once you begin to see the tail of your fish frequently breaking the surface then that is a sure sign that the fish is tiring and you should choose the best place in the pool or near where you are standing to land the fish. Guide your fish as near to your chosen spot as you can, and then increase the pressure to pull the head of the fish out of the water. Again this is a common fault with beginners who often do not pull the head of the fish up enough, and I can remember many anxious moments acting as netsman to young fishermen, unable to get a clear view of a beaten fish in the dark waters of Highland rivers because they were not lifting the salmon high enough in the water. The ideal way to proceed is to shorten your line and then lift and at the same time swing the fish into the landing place which should all be accomplished in one smooth movement. Always shorten your line first so that you don't have to reel in any more or worse still are tempted to handline at the vital moment, because any loss of pressure at this time can mean another run on the part of the fish.

There are four ways of landing a salmon, all of which you can do on your own but there is no doubt that some are much easier if you have a companion.

The first way which is much the best if you are on your own and, if conditions are suitable is really to beach your fish. Many people think that salmon can really only be beached if you have a gradually shelving gravelly beach on to which the fish can be pulled. Well this of course is ideal, but there are many pools which have a grassy bank, a little bay, or even one flat stone by the water's edge where salmon can be successfully beached.

The procedure is extremely simple. Play your fish until it is pretty dead and then choose a suitable spot. Walk the fish to this spot and then shortening your line swing it across the current until its head is out of the water and on to the landing place. Normally salmon will struggle when they first touch the bank but if you keep on an even pressure then the fish will soon cease to move and will lie inert on the beaching place. Then hold your rod in one hand well away from your body, slacken off enough line so that there isn't any acute strain on your rod tip, and at the same time keep sufficient pressure on the fish to prevent it slipping back into the pool. Walk down behind the fish and grasp it firmly around the wrist of its tail and lift it clear of the water. Do at all times remember that there is a strain on your rod tip otherwise you may be forcibly and expensively reminded by a nasty crack. Some anglers like to lift their fish by putting their fingers through the gills but in my opinion you run the risk of getting a hook in your fingers and it also makes the fish bleed. If you are in a really difficult place you can always reel up and put your rod down, making sure that the handle of your reel is facing upwards and then catch hold of the line and walk down to the fish, keeping a gentle pressure on the line to prevent the fish returning to the river. However don't do this unless you absolutely have to because if the fish does kick itself back into the river you are in trouble.

The next way of landing a fish is to net it. I find this an admirable way of landing a salmon if I am accompanied by a ghillie but I think it is an extremely awkward method if I am alone. Nevertheless I know many fishermen who do net their own salmon and there is no doubt that the modern light alloy collapsible nets which can easily be slung over your back have made life much more simple. If you are using a net then you must choose a place with deepish water close into the bank. Be careful that there are no obstructions underwater such as a large rock which will prevent the net being pushed under the fish at the vital moment. Once the fish is played out get your net ready for use and then holding the net underwater with one hand, draw the fish over the net, holding your rod in the other hand. It is important always to net your fish head first and immediately it is in the net lift the net out of the water. It is a good tip if you can to put a stone in the bottom of the net as then there is no risk of the fly being snagged by the floating mesh of the net which can easily pull the hook out of the fish's mouth.

The next method is to use a tailer which can work well but can be awkward. For those who don't know them a tailer is a device rather like a snare at the end of a long handle and it is set in a similar fashion. Again a tailer must be used in deep water. When you have played your fish out, you set the tailer if you are not carrying it preset and then slip it into the water over the fish's tail. Once the noose is over the tail a quick pull will trip the tailer and secure the noose round the tail of the fish. The trouble with tailers is that they can easily be set off by contact with any underwater obstruction and in that case you have to reset the tailer and start again. Perhaps it is worth saying that it is perfectly possible, if you are fishing a pool with a high bank which prevents you getting ashore, to tail a salmon by your hand. The only thing to note is that you really have to play your fish absolutely dead before you catch hold of the tail.

Netting a spring salmon on the Cassley

The last method of landing a fish is to gaff it. This used to be the most common method of landing a salmon but because it damages the flesh it has lost favour in recent years and is now even banned on some rivers. A gaff is nothing more than a sharp steel barbless hook and the telescopic gaffs were easily carried clipped to the angler's pocket. A gaff can be used equally well in deep or shallow water and there are some marvellous stories of ghillies, experts with the old-fashioned long handled gaff, who had salmon ashore within minutes of their being hooked. The best story being one of Patrick Chalmer's who tells of the 55 lb salmon being hauled ashore after only three minutes. If you are using a gaff by yourself then place the gaff point upwards under your fish and with a short, sharp movement impale the fish and draw the salmon out of the water. Once the fish is on the gaff it cannot kick itself off. Don't take a wild swipe with a gaff and don't gaff over the back of a fish for if you do so you increase the risk of gaffing the line instead of the salmon and the result will be disaster. Many coming fresh to salmon fishing may now never see a gaff used but if you are on your own it is still much the best instrument to help you when you are in an awkward place or dealing with a particularly heavy fish.

Finally everything is very much easier if you have an experienced helper with you. Most ghillies nowadays use a net and the best thing is to stand upstream of your assistant and then swing your fish across the current and into the net. Don't stand too close as otherwise you can become unsighted at the crucial moment and don't stand too far up the bank because this will lower the angle of your cast which can impede your ghillie as he goes to net your salmon or worse if you are fishing with a dropper which can catch in his clothes with one inevitable result.

Using a Ghillie

If you go to a river for the first time, no matter how experienced a fisherman you are, you will benefit enormously from the services of a ghillie. For every river is different. Fish lie in different places according to the height of the water and inhabit different pools in the different seasons of the year, and an experienced ghillie will know the lies, the flies that are preferred on the water and where the best taking places are likely to be.

I have often heard fishermen say glibly 'Oh I don't require a ghillie, I like to find things out for myself'. I think that such an attitude is foolish because it means that the angler will spend long periods of the day covering water where he has little chance of catching a fish, and even if he covers 20 yards of profitless water in each pool he will have greatly reduced his chances of catching the full potential of his beat.

An experienced ghillie who has spent a period of time on a beat of a river, will have had the priceless advantage of seeing the river at all heights of water, particularly when the water level is at its lowest. He will therefore have an intimate knowledge of the shape of the river bed, the depth of each pool, and over the years he will have built up a store of information of where fish are likely to be taken at each season and at all heights of water. There are other less obvious factors which influence a river. Some pools are affected by light, and will fish better in the morning or the afternoon. Some lies are best fished from the right bank and some from the left bank. Some pools require a larger or smaller size of fly. Some pools may look immensely attractive but have no real holding lies, and only fish well when fish are running or in the autumn. An experienced ghillie will know all these things and will be able to give the angler the benefit of all his wisdom, when, left to his own devices, he might fail to fish such a pool on the one occasion when

60

it was likely to be productive.

If you are lucky enough to be provided with a ghillie always make certain that you get the most out of what I am inclined to call a priceless asset. Don't be content simply to find out where to start at a pool and then allow the ghillie to go away. Ask him questions, such as 'where is the best lie in this pool?', 'am I fishing far enough across?', 'do I need to fish right into the bank?' Draw out all the information that the ghillie can impart and make certain that he knows that you are listening and paying attention to his advice.

It is a fishing truism that however accomplished a fisherman you are you can only be a real expert in water that you know intimately, and therefore when you go to a new river or beat for the first time you should make every effort to tap whatever expert knowledge is available to you. Many ghillies have a wealth of knowledge to impart and although some may appear to be dour and unfriendly if you show an interest you will learn not only a tremendous amount about the river but also about the wild life and possibly the history of the area.

Many ghillies as well are expert fishermen in their own right and given the chance they will give you advice on how to cast or on how to fish a pool which may appear on the face of it very difficult, but if it is tackled another way can in fact be fished quite easily.

Another thing. Don't be content only to learn what will apply to that day. Always ask your ghillie questions about other times of the year and different heights of water. You will often get the answer 'Oh we don't fish this pool in the summer' or 'that pool is only good during the grilse run or at the back-end' as the case may be. Or you may be told 'this pool is always good but later on in the year it fishes best from the other side'. All these little hints will be lost to you if you don't ask the question and you never know if you may be lucky enough to fish that water again, possibly at a different time of year, possibly without a ghillie, when such tips will prove invaluable.

Any young fisherman should keep a record book and all fish, no matter where they are caught should be entered. This record should include the river, the beat, the pool, the fly, the size of fly, the height of the water, the weight of the fish, the water temperature and the time of the day the fish was caught. If in the remarks column you also enter the place in the pool your record book will be perfect and serve you in good stead if you only fish a certain beat a few times in your life. If before returning to the beat you reread your book you will be able to refresh your memory with information long since forgotten and that can often mean the difference of one or two fish extra in the bag.

Finally no matter how well you know a river don't forget that the character of a river can change due to winter spates, ice and bank erosion and the planting or felling of trees. Some pools can lose a large proportion of their holding capacity just because one tree which provided shade has been blown down or washed away, while I know one well-known pool on the Naver which has become much less productive since the forestry plantations which surround it have grown up and now mask the pool from the wind, which formerly ruffled the tail which was the most productive area of the pool.

Salmon Taking Times

This is one of the most complex aspects of all salmon fishing and to pretend that one knows the real answer is quite wrong. Indeed salmon fishing is so uncertain that I can only say one thing definitely, which is you won't catch a fish if your fly is not in the water. And if you are an occasional salmon fisher who has one fishing holiday a year then you must just keep on casting and if conditions are bad, hope that you will meet with the proverbial 'daft yin'.

But in spite of this I think it can help to know when salmon are likely to take and many years of observation have shown me that the single most important factor is to have an air/water temperature gap where the air temperature is higher than the water. Why this is so important is extremely difficult to explain. I think probably it has something to do with the amount of dissolved oxygen in the water but I don't know. What I do know is that for good fly fishing you really need to have the air temperature 5°F higher than the water, and you may have some success when the gap is only 1 or 2°F, even if they are the same you can get the odd fish. But when the water is warmer than the air then you are most unlikely to catch anything. The old fishing rhyme was written very much with this in mind:

> When the wind is in the south
> Doth blow fly into fish's mouth.
> When the wind is in the west
> 'Tis now that fishing's at its best
> When the wind is in the east
> 'Tis not fit for man nor beast
> When the wind is in the north
> The careful fisher goes not forth.

Indeed if a north wind is blowing, unless the water temperatures are below 40°F then you are very unlikely to get air temperatures that are higher than those of the water.

When therefore are we likely to find this gap most favourable? Speaking generally, in the early months of the year, particularly in the Highland rivers whose catchment areas are surrounded by high mountains, and in January, February and March, it is rare, except in periods of prolonged frost to have an air/water temperature gap that is other than favourable. The temperature of the water is kept below 40°F by the melting snow on the hills and in these months you can get ideal angling conditions with high clear rivers. There are two proven times of the day which are more likely to be successful at this time of the year. Firstly the period between 11am and 1pm at which time the air temperature is generally at its highest and secondly between 3–5pm. If the nights are cold with temperatures below freezing point then as the air warms up during the day the snow on the hills will melt and this will make the river rise just a little late in the afternoon and it is this reason, I think, which makes this late afternoon period so profitable on some rivers.

As the year progresses into April and May and the days become longer and warmer, the water temperature will start to rise fairly rapidly. In years where there has been little snow on the hills this will occur earlier in the year, if there has been a lot of snow, and sometimes snow can persist on the Scottish Highlands into May and June, then the water temperature will rise more slowly. It is in the summer period of the year that you will often find a very very small air/water temperature gap or even a reverse gap with the water being warmer than the air and this is why anglers are so often unsuccessful even when conditions are, on the face of it, ideal.

As May goes on into June the water temperature rises rapidly through the 50°s and often into the mid and upper 60°s F. At this time of year it is often very difficult to get a clear gap between the air and water temperature and indeed if the wind is cold the gap is invariably the wrong way. In my opinion as I explain fully in the chapter on summer fishing the energetic angler will fish from dawn until 9.30am and then again in the evening. These are the times which offer the best hope of success. Also remember that the weather affects the places in a pool where the fish will lie. In very cold weather, and similarly in very hot weather, fish will move out of the shallower, streamy runs, and rest in the deeper, stiller parts of the pool. This is especially true in the summer when the sun is beating down on the surface of the water. Because fish lying in the deep still waters are almost impossible to catch unless there is a good wind to ruffle the water, you should fish when they are likely to be on the move. On very cold days if the air temperature rises, then they will move back into the shallower parts of the stream, and conversely on hot days when the sun sets they will move up into the runs preparatory to moving up river during the night. In both these cases this is likely to be in the evening.

Another imponderable factor which can, indeed does, influence the likely taking times of salmon is light. The rivers most affected by light are those which flow through deep gorges and on rivers like this, if there is any heavy cloud cover then, conditions may well be hopeless. Even on more open rivers you can get some lights that will favour one bank rather than the other but it is not possible to know, or even take account of the conditions of light, without expert local knowledge. Perhaps like many things in salmon fishing factors such as light, and indeed all factors, air/water temperature gap, the height of the river are largely irrelevant because it is not within the power of man to change these things, but personally I find it a comfort to be able to explain success, or lack of it, and I hope that others may think the same way.

There are some weather conditions that are definitely either favourable or unfavourable. First of all in the spring if it is snowing then the fishing is likely to be excellent. Generally the air temperature usually rises quite sharply once snow starts to fall and I think that this is the reason why fishing in a snowstorm is usually so good but it may be that there is some trick of the light which is also a helpful factor. On the other hand there are certain times when you might as well pack up and go home. The first of these is when mist rises from the river: if you are fishing in the evening in the summer and this happens, go back to bed. I am tempted to use the words of Monopoly 'Do not pass Go, Do not collect £200.' You won't catch anything. Secondly again usually in the summer if the weather is thundery, find something else to do. I have hardly ever known fish caught on dull oppressive thundery days and most experts would agree with me.

Once the thunderstorm has broken then fish may take well but this is not a certainty. Thirdly, many fishermen I know feel that it is not worth fishing when the barometer is dropping dramatically. I must confess that I haven't noticed this myself but I admit that I could have

Fishing before a gathering storm, Loch Ailsh

overlooked it. Finally if rain is falling in very heavy drops on the water then again in my opinion you are unlikely to catch anything. Whether this is because inevitably rivers start to rise in these conditions or because the heavy drops distort the salmon's view of the fly I am not sure, but in any case conditions like this generally last but so short a time that it cannot be said to be a general hazard.

So far I know I have talked only of weather conditions and the way these affect the likelihood of catching salmon. Of course the other main factor is the water level.

There is absolutely no doubt that on most rivers the best fishing conditions are when the river is falling steadily. A rising river, particularly if it is rising rapidly, generally is hopeless. There is however a magical moment when the river starts to rise for the first time following a period of low water conditions. Then fish will take all over the river and I have often seen several rods playing a fish at once, hooked just on the rise. But this period lasts so short a time that often you miss it because you are not covering a fish when it occurs and by the time you have landed your fish generally it is over. The other time when a rising river is beneficial as I have said is in the spring when melting snow causes the river to rise in the afternoon. But I think it is difficult to say how long this lasts as often the rise does not occur until the evening when darkness is falling.

As I have said if the river is rising fast and particularly in the summer and autumn when there is a large amount of debris coming down, then conditions generally are hopeless. If the river is rising slowly then you may get the odd fish but I have noticed that salmon often come short on a rising river and it is common for more fish to be pulled and lost than landed. Once the river steadies and starts to fall then fish begin to take more freely and it is then that good catches are obtained.

Most anglers when they see a good flow of water in the river tend to put on bigger flies, and I think that in the spring this is the right thing to do. But in summer spate conditions I am sure that most fishermen fish much too big. I know myself that I am guilty of this and this point was forcibly brought home to me two years ago when I went to fish a neighbouring river in full spate conditions at the end of May. I had a tube fly about an inch long on my cast and when I arrived the ghillie took me to look at it and asked me to change it for a microscopic blue/black tube about ¼ inch long to which he attached a size 16 silver treble. My initial reaction was that this was far too small for the prevailing conditions but that I had better show willing and at least try it to start with. In fact I ended up by keeping it on all day during which I killed 9 fish most of which were stale. I could argue that I would have done as well with my original fly but I doubt it for I am sure that some would have fluffed at the bigger fly.

Finally just to show that there is an exception to every rule let me tell the story of two consecutive days that occurred on the Cassley early in April 1956. March had been completely dry and by the end of it the river was at the low summer level of 6 inches. On the Sunday night it started to rain and on Monday rain was still falling heavily. We went out to fish an obviously rising river and to my surprise the salmon took solidly all day and we landed 34 fish which at that time was our record bag for a day. During the day the river rose from 2 foot 3 inches to 5 foot 6 inches. The Tuesday morning the river had dropped back to 2 foot 6 inches but the rain came down again and the river rose all day, but again fish took voraciously and we ended the day with 35 on the bank, beating the previous record by one. During this period the river again rose by 3 feet. I have fished the Cassley for 45 years and I have never ever seen fish take like that on a rising river either before or since those remarkable two days.

The Choice of Fly

I would say that of all things in salmon fishing nothing causes more worry and concern than the choice of fly, and in the olden days when there were hundreds of patterns available the difficulty must indeed have seemed perplexing. However I do not think it is a subject on which I wish to be dogmatic.

Size is much, much more important than pattern and I think that, while as in all things in salmon fishing, there are exceptions, the only really important thing is to fish with a pattern of fly in which you have confidence. To prove this to myself, one year I fished with nothing except a Mar Lodge which I carried in every available size and my catch at the end of the year was almost identical with my 10 year average of rod-caught fish. Arthur Wood fished the whole of one year 'for a bet' with a March Brown, he tells us that he caught his share 'and more' of the total catch. So I really don't think that pattern is very important. But I will say that if you don't think the fly you are using will catch fish, then you won't catch any, even if that fly is successful elsewhere in the river. Why this should be I don't know but I am sure it is a fact.

In the spring when the water temperature is below 42° then you must fish with a fly 2½–6 inches in length or if you are fishing with a weighted fly and are trying to sink it to the level of the fish a fly of over 1 inch. In the early part of the year I think you should fish with a brightish fly, either one of the old authentic patterns such as a Jock Scott, or if you are fishing with one of the modern long tailed flies a Tadpole, which has a maroon head and a red and yellow body. From March–June during the smolt run I find silver bodied flies most effective. Here perhaps I should say that I think that the colour of the body is in my opinion much more important than the dressing and I

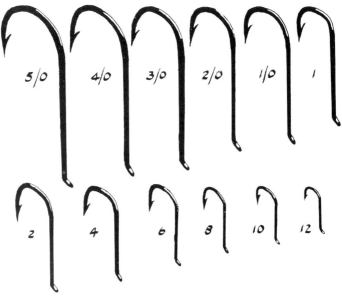

Sizes of salmon hooks

think it is the body of the fly reflecting rays of light as it turns and twists in the current during its traverse across the pool that alerts and attracts the fish. During the smolt run I think that the Silver Grey, Mar Lodge and Dusty Miller are my favourite patterns and as I have already said I would rather fish with a Mar Lodge than any other pattern of fly.

In April and May as the trees come into full leaf I think that some of the brighter patterns of fly are at their most effective, flies such as the Green Highlander, a good fly at all times, Gordon, Poynder and Durham Ranger.

After the water temperature has reached 42°F there is a period of transition, when the water temperature lies between 42–50°F. At these temperatures fish can be caught on a wide variety of fly sizes from sizes 8 and 9 up to flies 6 inches in length and it is at this time that it will pay the angler to change frequently and fish a pool as the old ghillie said 'with the "correct" size of fly followed by the sublime and then the ridiculous'.

After the water temperature reaches 50°F then, generally, salmon become much more choosy and take flies size 4–12 best. They will sometimes move to a larger fly but often fluff it instead of taking it

Traditional

Hair Winged

Double - hooked

Esmond Drury

Low Water

Waddington

Tube

Types of salmon fly

71

solidly. In the summer it pays to change from the bright patterns of the spring, to more drab coloured fly the pure black Stoat's Tail being a general favourite. Other good summer flies are Logie, Blue Charm, March Brown, Lady Caroline and Hairy Mary but if you have a favourite you should stick to it. In my opinion in the summer most people fish with flies that are too big. It is surprising how small a fly summer salmon prefer even in good water levels. For myself once the water temperature reaches 42°F then I always put on a size 9 Hairy Mary on my dropper which I don't change and content myself with ringing the changes on my tail fly. Even in a spate few anglers on the Hope fish with flies bigger than size 12, and I have known countless occasions when the only angler fishing with very small flies in good or high water in summer has caught fish when all the others have been blank.

So in the summer I would use sombre flies in small sizes for preference. But I would always be prepared to change my fly and when I changed I would make a radical change both in size and pattern. In the autumn as the water temperatures start to drop salmon seem to prefer brighter coloured flies again and I have found that those with some orange such as a Willy Gunn, General Practitioner or Munro Killer most effective.

Having said that if you want to be more precise you can follow the advice of Richard Waddington who starts off fishing a size fly 4 when the water temperature is between 48–50°F and changes one size smaller for every 2° rise in the water temperature. And if you want to be more precise still you can buy a fly size calculator which takes into account the water temperature, the speed of the current and the water level, and you can dial up the correct size of fly for the pool you are going to fish. But if you don't want to be so scientific then you can rely on the old adages 'a bright fly for a bright day, and a dull fly for a dull day', and 'suit the size of fly to the height of the water'. Neither of these two sayings are great favourites of mine. The only guidelines I do believe in are that very often in high and peat stained water a gold bodied fly such as a Dunkeld can be effective and that the colour of the fly does depend far more on the terrain and light conditions on a particular river than on the brightness or dullness of the day.

But there is no doubt that on occasions, and in my experience these are very rare, the pattern of fly does really matter though why this should be I don't know. I remember once going to fish the Laxford in the summer. The ghillie told me I should put on a shrimp which was the favoured fly but I did not have a shrimp pattern in my fly box so I put on a rather maroon dressing of an Usk Grub that someone had given me. Immediately I caught several fish but the hooks must have been faulty because the first and then a second one broke in a fish. These were the only two flies I had of this pattern so the ghillie then returned to his house to get a shrimp fly but I never touched another fish after that and I can only put it down to that precise dressing which for some reason or other, probably a trick of the light, the fish wanted on that day.

There are definitely some days when a minimal change in the pattern of fly can make all the difference. I have known days when fish have been caught on a Black Doctor, but not a Hairy Mary or Stoat's Tail and vice versa – and therefore I think it does pay to change your fly, and change it fairly frequently if you are not at first successful. Not forgetting that it also pays to change the way you fish, fishing the fly faster or slower, backing up a pool, or in the summer fishing with the floating line and letting the fly hang in the current to imitate plankton.

Spring Fishing

Spring fishing for salmon is in many ways a euphemistic, certainly often an optimistic, term for much of it is done in extreme wintry conditions but forgetting the weather, the salmon fisherman who goes forth in the months of January, February, March and April is hoping to catch fish that have entered the river after the closing date of the previous season or are fresh run from the sea, all of which are due to spawn in October or November of that year.

People forget that there are four distinct runs of salmon in Scotland, spring, summer, autumn, and winter, with the winter run entering the river systems from October onwards to spawn a year later. On rivers like the Tay where many autumn fish are killed it would be perfectly possible in early October to catch two fresh fish on the same day, one of which was going to spawn within a few weeks, and one of which was going to spawn a year later. It is only because most rivers are quite rightly rested from October or mid-October until the middle of January or the beginning of February, that more is not heard of the winter run of fish and on certain rivers like the Aberdeenshire Dee and Tay which have a significant number of fish entering their systems during those months, the opening days of the season are often extremely productive because the angler is covering a number of salmon that have not seen any sort of lure before and these fish are often distributed over a large part of the river system.

Traditionally spring fishing for salmon on the bigger river systems is associated with spinning and there are few fishermen who given the choice would fish with a fly rather than spin. For myself with one important proviso, I would always fish with a fly and I would expect to catch as many salmon as anyone spinning, provided I could cover the water sufficiently. In other words if I was fishing on the lower

74

River Oykel, Ross-shire

beats of the Tweed in the spring and I had access to a boat then I would fish with a fly and only if I was stuck on the bank where I could cover 30 more yards of water each cast with a minnow would I spin.

It is worth considering that in the north of Scotland where by agreement with the proprietors a fly only rule prevails, the Kyle of Sutherland rivers, the Oykel, Cassley, Shin and Carron, together with the Helmsdale and Thurso open on the 11th January which is earlier than any other rivers in Scotland and they are closely followed by the Naver which opens on the 12th January. Given an open winter with the rivers free from excessive ice, and I should say that in a hard winter they can be almost totally frozen over for the months of January and February, it is quite common for the rod catch to be over 200 fish in these rivers by the end of March, all caught on the fly and this on rivers which compared to the Spey, Dee and Tay are extremely short with relatively little fishing.

I have heard it said that sunk line fishing in the spring is merely an inefficient form of spinning. But this is not the case and the fly does have certain advantages, particularly nowadays when modern rods, lines and flies make fishing relatively easy compared with the 16–18 foot Greenheart or split cane rods and meat hooks of flies that were wielded by our forefathers.

So let me take you to the river in February and March, and let us see what we find and how we should proceed. I will be optimistic and assume that conditions are good, the river will be swollen by the melting snow on the hills, the water will be cold from 35–37°F and the wind will be west with cloud cover and the air temperature will be 42°F rising to 45°F in the afternoon. The height of the river and clarity of the water are one of the main features of spring fishing – the melting snow on the hills not only makes the river an ideal height but the colder nights keep the water temperature down well below the air temperature and that as I cannot stress too frequently creates ideal angling conditions.

I will fish with a slow sinking line pausing for a moment to mourn the passing of the old dressed silk Kingfisher lines which were undoubtedly the finest ever made for spring fishing. I will use a heavy nylon leader of 20 lbs breaking strain or more and I will put a 2½ inch tube fly on the end of my cast. There is no doubt that the slow sinking line is much the best to use in the spring. A line which just has a sinking tip will not let you sink the fly low enough in the water in streamy places and a fast sinking line goes down too deep, too quickly, which results in your fly continually snagging rocks, and also has other disadvantages which I will come to in a moment.

Always fish a light fly to start with and aim to swim your fly between 9 and 15 inches below the surface. The reason for this is that you want to make the fish come up to you as if he does he will be moving more quickly and therefore takes solidly, on the other hand if he misses the fly the chances are that you will see a movement on the surface which allows you to try the fish again. The way to keep the fly at this depth is by handlining, maintaining contact with the fly at all times, exactly as I have outlined in my chapter on Fly Fishing.

Now let us assume that you are unlucky and you do not move a fish. Don't change your fly but back the pool up and very often this will produce a take. If that doesn't work then put on a bigger fly; say 4 inches in length and fish the pool down again and if that doesn't work then leave the pool and pass on to the next one. If, however, that pool is a holding pool of good repute it is well worth returning later in the day to fish it again and on that occasion you should fish a weighted fly first and if that fails to attract a fish as a last resort you should then back it up with a 6 inch long tailed fly such as a Collie Dog or Tadpole.

When you fish a weighted fly you are really trying to get your fly down close to the depth at which the fish are lying in the pool. To do this you must cast fairly square across the river and forget about the belly in your line and let the fly work very slowly across the river until you handline in at the end of the cast to make the fly buoyant enough to cast again. Never use a very large fly when you are doing this, a 2 inch tube is quite big enough and you are trying to sink your fly from 2–5 feet in the river according to the nature of the pool. This method which I admit is a form of spinning with a fly rod does work on occasions. It usually works best in very blustery conditions, in the faster currents or when there is a very narrow air/water temperature gap, but when you fish like this you are sacrificing the visibility of the fly to the fish against the sky which is the main advantage of fly fishing and you should not fish your pool in this way until other methods have failed, unless you are faced with exceptionally cold conditions combined with high water flows.

I have seen some fishermen in the spring who always use weighted flies fishing under the impression that they must always try and get the fly down to the fish. But on many occasions they fail to do this because they cast at too acute an angle downstream and hold their rod tips too high. If you are getting the fly down to the fish you must make the conscious decision to change your method of presentation, cast square or pretty square across the river and hold the point of your rod down to the water to give the fly time to sink.

Of course, as in all salmon fishing, you will not always have perfect conditions. If the river is very high then you can start off with a tube fly of around 4 inches in length and work up to one of 6 inches in length, but it is a mistake to fish your biggest fly first however high the river. In the spring salmon will lie generally in deep quiet moving water, or anywhere behind a large stone or boulder that creates a lie in the stream. You will find them in the tails of pools, particularly if there is a long rapid below the pool, and beside the current at the head of the pool but not generally in the neck unless they are running or on a very mild evening. In very high water they will come close into the bank away from the direct force of the stream and then you must be sure to fish your fly right into the bank, swinging the rod in and then out. Never if you can avoid it let the rod tip come into a direct line with the fly.

The other conditions you get in the spring are a prolonged period of cold, dry frosty weather, when the water level will drop away and ice will form on the edges of the stream. These are without a doubt the worst possible conditions because the fish will tend to drop back into the dead water. There will be insufficient current to fish the correct size of fly properly, and if you fish a sunk fly with a quick sinking line you will invariably get snagged in the low water conditions. If you are unfortunate enough to meet conditions of this sort it is worth changing to a floating line, or a floating line with a sinking tip and a long leader, and it is even worth trying a fly size 5 or 6 first time down the pool and then changing to the largest size of fly that the water flow will enable you to swim properly. Under these conditions it is best to fish your pools carefully and often ringing the change of flies and fly size you use and possibly because of melting snow on the hills the river may just rise an inch or two from 3pm onwards. Most fish in these conditions are caught in the last two hours of daylight provided frost is not falling. There is however one time when in these conditions you can confidently expect success. If you get a good upstream wind that ruffles the surface of the dead water, then all the water that has been unfishable for days can be backed up and you can suit the size of the fly to the height of the wave. When this happens you will very often have the chance of success and on occasions an excellent day's sport because for the first time for days you will be presenting the fly properly to fish that may not have seen a fly for some time.

One of the big surprises of fishing in the spring is how well fish will take in a snowstorm and often I have seen fish taking freely when snow has reduced the visibility to less than 20 yards, and you would have thought that the fish could hardly have seen the fly. The reason for this I think as I have said is that the air temperature inevitably warms up when it starts to snow, which creates a bigger air/water temperature gap. Another thing that I find surprising is the best time of day. Reading Lord Grey's book *Fly Fishing* I was interested to note that he remarked on March weather fishing on the Helmsdale where when it was frosty and the sun was strong the river would rise a few inches in the afternoon '. . . in consequence we invariably hooked one or two salmon at the same hour in the afternoon. As long as the frost lasted, this was the only good hour of the day, but it was a certainty.'

After mild winters or in the late spring once the snow has melted water temperatures can rise appreciably, well above 40°F, therefore you must be prepared under these conditions to try a wider range of fly sizes in all heights of water. It is now that a floating line with a sinking tip comes into its own and can be very productive with a fly range varying according to conditions from ½–1½ inches, and in exceptionally mild weather and low water flows a full floating line with even smaller flies is worth a try. However, large flies fished on a slow sinking line will still account for the majority of fish even under these circumstances and are especially productive when used with the backing up technique. It is perhaps the most opportune period for you to carry two rods equipped with different lines and flies to enable you to try both options. At these temperatures fish will favour the heads of pools and streamy water in low flows, but in higher flows can be found throughout the pool with the tail of the pools usually well inhabited. These haunts can be very productive.

On the rivers I know best – the Cassley and the Oykel – the best time for the Cassley is the first fishing of a pool in the morning, while on the Oykel, next door so to speak, the majority of fish are caught from 3pm onwards in the afternoon. And different weather conditions favour different rivers. In the spring on both the Cassley and the Oykel a dullish day is best, while the Brora, a little further to the east, fishes best on a bright sunny day. Why these differences occur is difficult to explain; it may be something to do with the intensity of light, but whatever it is, it just illustrates how unpredictable salmon can be.

Summer Fishing

During the last twenty years summer fishing for salmon, in Scotland particularly, has been greatly improved by the increase in the number of salmon and grilse entering the rivers in June, July and August. And during the same period of years there has been a marked decrease in the spring run of fish. In many rivers in recent years the catches recorded between June and September have broken all records and these catches could well have been even higher had it not been for the long periods of drought during the summer months of the last few years.

There are two other factors which have had an effect on the salmon catches of recent years. First of all the great increase in illegal netting off the shores of Scotland which has accounted for a large number of salmon and grilse before they could enter the river systems. The second factor is the disease Ulcerative Dermal Necrosis known as UDN. It is extremely likely that this disease is the same as the salmon disease that occurred in the mid 1800s which was then named 'Bacillus Pestis'. Because the bacteriologists of that age could not identify the disease they gave it a descriptive name. Similarly modern virologists and bacteriologists have been unable to identify the disease and have named it descriptively. It is a pity that they did not adopt the original name but one can only assume that they were unsure whether the disease was caused by a virus or a bacillus. At the start of the disease large numbers of salmon and sea trout died but recently the mortality rate seems to be declining. However where it is present, and there are few rivers without any sign of the disease, it does have a marked effect on the angling catches. It appears to me that where the disease is present in a fish's system at all, even to a small degree, the fish become lethargic and very difficult to catch except under the most ideal of angling conditions. I have observed that while reasonable catches can be made when everything is right immediately conditions deteriorate catches immediately show a marked decline and in low water when the disease is present in a river they become almost impossible to catch on a fly. Another point of interest is that the disease seems to affect the bigger fish more than the smaller.

This increase in the number of fish running in the summer could only be a temporary swing in the pattern of nature and could be reversed just as quickly as it came about. But it is worth examining some of the possible causes as to why this should have happened. Some people believe that the Greenland netting is the cause. The argument is that it is the spring and winter running salmon who winter off Greenland, and if a large proportion of them are netted in the high seas then the spring run automatically declines. Another theory is that better river management, in particular the opening-up of unpopulated feeding tributaries has benefited the summer fish, while a third theory is that the majority of hatchery planted fry produce summer fish. This may or may not be the case and it could well be that one or all of these factors have played some part in bringing about this change. My own view however is that such a significant cyclical change can only be accounted for by some phenomenon which has taken place in the feeding and spawning grounds in our rivers.

There is absolutely no doubt that the stock of salmon in a salmon river is largely controlled by two factors. Firstly the amount of spawning gravel in the river system, and secondly the amount of feeding available for the fry and parr in the river and its spawning tributaries. If there is a limited amount of spawning gravel available then the redds cut by the early runs of fish, the first fish to spawn, will be recut by the later spawning summer and on occasions autumn fish. This results in a heavy loss to the ova of the early runs. Likewise if the feeding capacity of the river system is overcrowded too many weak fry and parr will be produced instead of a smaller number of well-fed fish. If the smolts leaving the river in the spring are weak, then they will not travel so far and they then will return after only one sea winter as grilse the following June.

In my opinion the very wet summers of the middle and late '50s allowed too many summer salmon and grilse through the coastal and river netting stations, which resulted in overcrowding of the spawning beds. Also the beds themselves have been threatened by soil erosion caused by forestry and land drainage which silts up the gravel. And this is the real reason behind this cyclical swing from spring to summer runs. I have noted that just recently following the drought years of the early '70s there has been an increase in the number of spring fish which would support this theory.

Whatever the cause many fishermen prefer to fish in the summer, not only because of the increased number of fish over the last ten years but also because of the pleasant weather which means that non-fishing wives can accompany their husbands and enjoy the pleasant sur- roundings of the river bank or drive round and see the magnificent scenery.

Summer fishing, however, from an angling point of view does have its problems. The main problem is that the water conditions generally depend entirely on rainfall and if there is no rain, which there may well not be then there is no, or very little water to fish in. On the bigger east coast rivers with a large catchment area, the Aberdeen- shire Dee, the Spey, the Tay, water levels may remain perfectly adequate until well on in June, provided that there has been sufficient snowfall the previous winter. Other rivers, particularly the Helmsdale, Alness, Thurso and Inver have man-made barriers built on the bigger lochs at the top of their catchment areas to store the winter and spring rainfall and snow-melt so that it can be released during the summer months to augment the natural flow. Other rivers have been harnessed to provide hydro-electric power and where the generating stations have been built some distance from the river mouths and liberal com- pensation flows were agreed before the completion of the schemes, these rivers are assured of better flows during drought periods than they would normally have enjoyed. Among the rivers to benefit in this way are the Tay, Tummel, Awe, Beauly, Conon, Shin, Garry and Morriston. Other rivers however have their catchment areas tapped and so they lose a valuable part of their flow during high water conditions. Among rivers to suffer in this way are the Lyon, Brora, Cassley and Carron.

The rivers of the west coast of Scotland generally have only a sparse spring run and the main bulk of the salmon coming into these rivers does not arrive until early June. July, August and September have always been the best fishing months on the west coast. Also many of these rivers and the Ewe, Gruiniards, and Laxford are excellent examples having large lochs at the head of their catchment areas which act as natural reservoirs. These lochs not only augment the

Fishing on the River Dee

natural flows but themselves provide excellent fishing when the rivers are too low and in some cases are preferred by the angler who likes to fish from a boat. Many of these rivers as well have an excellent run of sea trout from June onwards which coincide with the main salmon run and fish from 10–20 lbs in weight are caught annually.

When fishing in the summer if you are lucky enough to have good water conditions especially during late-May and June, then there is little difference between summer and late spring fishing. The water temperature, particularly if there is still snow melting on the hills, will be in the high 40°s to mid 50°s F, and the air temperature should be appreciably higher than this. This provides ideal angling conditions. The size of fly will range from 1 to 10 or even larger according to the height and temperature of the water, and the angler will be able to fish in comfort using a 12–14 foot rod with a floating line or a sinking tip.

However if normal summer conditions apply with little or no rainfall at the end of the snow melt then the river will drop rapidly and the temperature of the water will rise. It is not impossible to catch fish under such conditions and with a little care and thought all is by no means lost. First of all, for the fisherman who is accompanied by his wife and family, or who is getting on in years and prefers to fish the normal hours of 9am to 6pm, concentrate on covering as much of your water as you can in the morning. Salmon run and move their lies during the night and fish that have moved pools overnight will often be found resting in the streamy runs at the heads of pools, in quicker draws in narrow parts of a pool or in the tail the next morning. Provided you fish your water with care, which means not getting too close to the water, and use light tackle and a wise choice of fly, then there is no reason not to expect success. In the morning many of the pools will be shaded from the direct rays of the sun, and you should take care to fish the most exposed pools on the beat first and then move quickly on to the more shaded pools on your beat. I firmly believe that the first fly down the pool is the best chance and therefore it makes sense to cover as much of your beat as you can before the sun's rays are shining directly down-river. Another point I believe is that if you catch a fish, then don't as some anglers do rest the pool, start again immediately and you will be surprised how often you get another fish in the next few casts. If you rest the pool you are merely losing precious fishing time which in sunny weather and drought conditions is scarce.

On bright sunny days in the summer by about 2pm the sun is in a position to shine directly down the majority of the (east coast) rivers of Scotland and conversely it shines directly down the west coast rivers from about 11am for about four hours. This has two effects. The heat of the sun's rays reflected on the water make any fish lying in the shallow streamy runs in the river uncomfortable. They then either sink deeper in the water or they drop back into the deeper, stiller parts of the pool, generally where there is insufficient stream to work the fly properly. In either case they are that much more difficult to attract to the fly and only if there is a rock or tree to shade their lie will they remain at a takeable depth.

The other effect is that fish are looking directly into the sun which either prevents them seeing it or if they can see it when they move to the fly are no doubt faced with the same difficulties as the fielder trying to catch a skier in the outfield directly into the sun's rays, and they are practically blinded at the vital moment. I have often seen ardent anglers trying to combat such conditions with their finest tackle. They would do better to consider the angle of the various pools on their beat and confine their efforts to those least affected by the sun, or better still rest the river until later in the day.

Of course if the weather is cool and cloudy then it is worth fishing on right through the day, but even then the morning is most likely to be the best time. Another exception is if there is a strong wind blowing, preferably upstream. If your beat contains a number of large holding pools with little or no current running through them then a strong wind will produce a pronounced wave. After an hour or two this seems to stir up the fish and they begin to porpoise and show on the surface. These pools are ideal for backing up or alternatively, if the current allows you, you can fish these pools exactly like a loch casting with the wind and working against it either upstream or downstream and handlining to work the fly. One of the best examples of this type of water is the Long Pool on the Cassley which extends for a mile in length and at low water has no current running through it at all. In this particular pool fish can be caught anywhere down the whole length but if you are fishing a pool of this type you should always take care to cover any place where you see a fish move. Even a faint ripple can sometimes produce a fish in the still deep parts of a pool and if the current is a worry then you should correct it by handlining faster.

If you are untrammelled by personal or domestic considerations then without a doubt the best time to fish in the summer months is the early morning between sunrise and breakfast. This is true at all heights of water but it is particularly true when the river is low and conditions are unfavourable. There are two reasons for this. Firstly the sun will not have reached the water and any fish that has moved up in the night will still be lying at the top of the streams and these present the best chance of success. Secondly this is the time of day when the air/water temperature ratio is likely to be at its most favourable. I cannot stress too much how important this difference is and how even a difference of one degree can mean a noticeable difference in the taking habits of salmon. The water temperature will have dropped overnight and the air will rapidly grow warmer as the sun comes over the horizon. Only on mornings when there is a tinge of frost in the air or when the north wind is blowing will this not be the case.

Even if you have fished your beat before breakfast then it is worthwhile returning to fish out the morning because another good taking time can be between 12 and 2pm. And many experienced anglers either do not have their lunch until after 2pm or stagger their lunch hour so that their beat is fished during that period.

Then if I was you, I would rest the beat until the evening, a time which nearly all authorities recommend. Evening fishing can be very productive.

Chaytor in *Letters to a Salmon Fisher's Sons* says that 'after a hot glaring day in August or September the hour of sunset or twilight is never without hope and may often prove most deadly. Many and many a time have I known two, three or four fish to be taken in this hour by a rod that had moved nothing all day. But too often the fisher has gone home to dinner at the very time when he should be fishing the hardest. The best chance lasts but a short time and comes after sunset, when the light has failed so much that the surface of the water seems to reflect it all, and you seem to be casting into a river of liquid metal. On such hopeless days you should keep your likeliest spots for the last few casts in the failing light, and should be careful to disturb the fish there as little as possible during the afternoon.' Excellent advice.

I think that the reason why evening fishing can be so productive in the summer is because as dusk approaches and the air cools fish that had sheltered from the heat of the day in the depths of the pool, start once more, to move up into the streams. Certainly the air/water temperature gap is unlikely to be as favourable. But one word of warning. Evening fishing does not suit every pool, particularly those in deep gorges or closed in by heavy wooded country or steep banks. And this I imagine is due more to bad visibility than any other reason.

If you are fishing on a river which has a run of sea trout then you can often have good sport in low water in the evening. Local knowledge is invaluable when fishing for sea trout but as a general rule you should concentrate on the glides at the tails of pools and wait until you see the bats start to fly before you start fishing. Sea trout, unlike salmon, need to feed when they are in the river, and where they are present can be a satisfactory way of saving the blank.

If I am fishing in the summer in the early morning or evening then I use the same size of fly that I would normally use during the day. Some fishermen put on a bigger fly in the evening as they feel that it is easier for the fish to see. There may be some truth in this, especially in gorgy pools where the salmon may not view the fly against the background of the sky, but I think in general that fishermen use too large flies in the summer, especially when the river is at a good height.

Anglers fishing in the early morning and evening have the added attraction of fishing when the countryside is at its most peaceful. There is the chance of seeing an otter fishing his water and the red deer come down from the hills to drink as dusk falls. However fishing at these times does have two disadvantages, one of which can be dealt with and one which can't. The first of these is mist. Once mist starts rising off the water in the evening then the wise fisherman will go home to his bed, and similarly in the morning, he will wait until the mist clears before starting to fish. The second disadvantage in Scotland is the midge which particularly on damp airless days can cause such a torment that fishing becomes virtually impossible. Only the bravest can endure the Highland midge but often the fishing can be good in the midgiest of conditions. There is the lovely story of an intrepid old lady who was fishing the Helmsdale with a very opinionated ghillie. The day was very midgy and the ghillie was in favour of going home. However the old lady covered her head with an old silk scarf in which she cut two small holes to see through, donned an old pair of silk gloves, and proceeded to catch three fish in the afternoon. Every time that the ghillie who had taken refuge in the car had to climb out and land another fish the air became bluer and bluer, and not just with tobacco smoke.

I think that statistically the angler who confines his fishing to the early morning and late evening during the summer is likely to be just as successful as the fisherman who spends all day by the water. My late father who fished on the Welsh Dee used to fish before and after

Laxford Bridge

work during the summer and on a three rod beat, his tally at the end of the season was usually about half the total bag. Another interesting thing is that he was a fly fishing purist while the other anglers who fished the beat used to spin and also fish both the prawn and shrimp in the summer.

Summer fishing can have one or two disadvantages. Thunder is one of them and from my experience is absolutely fatal. I have hardly ever known a fish caught when thunder is in the air although once the thunderstorm has arrived and the atmosphere has cleared then they can often take quite well. Another, and this really only applies to the lower beats of the large east coast rivers, is weed growth. Where these rivers flow through arable land and the fertiliser is washed into the river, the ranunculus and water buttercup really can impede the caster, and also if he is not careful cost him a good many flies and often a fish that is being played. Further up the river where the banks are fringed with trees there is a short period in the early summer when the trees come into leaf and the bud sheaths are blown onto the surface of the water. This is a confounded nuisance for the angler for not only is he constantly catching the bud sheaths on his fly, but more importantly the fish get lulled by the constant procession of objects floating over their heads and are very unlikely to take the floating fly normally presented. The only chance for the fisherman confronted with this is to put on a sinking line or a sinking tip and fish his fly deeper in the water below the surface and work it fairly fast to make a contrast to the sheaths' movement.

After the end of the snow melt the first spate will bring a complete change to the clarity of the water in most Highland rivers, especially if they flow through moorland and peaty areas. The water will turn brown often as dark as beer and this will have the effect of making the fish sick. When this happens I think that you should pay careful attention to the pattern of fly that you are using and I have found that the best to use are those with gold tinsel in the body, like Dunkeld, Thunder and Lightning or Hairy Mary. Other people have found black flies in particular the Sweep and Stoat's Tail very effective, as they show up most clearly against the sky while many people favour very bright flies with a lot of yellow in them such as the Garry Dog, Yellow Torrish or Green Highlander. As I have said before I think that you should use the pattern of fly in which you have confidence.

Once the water temperature rises above 45°F I start using a dropper and I would recommend that all fishermen should do the same. The only exception I would make is if you are fishing in a river where there is a lot of weed. The advantages of using a dropper are that it is a useful way of giving the salmon the choice of two flies in one fishing of a pool, and also I believe that there is a subtle difference in the way that the two flies are presented. If you do try a dropper you just fish in the normal way and forget about the dropper except that you should watch for a swirl rather closer towards you than the end of your cast. Some people never fish with a dropper because they say that if you hook a fish there is the risk of the spare fly catching on a rock or some other obstruction. This does sometimes happen but in my experience very, very seldom. If you hook a fish on the dropper nine times out of ten the tail fly will hook itself onto the cast above the hooked fish, after the fish has made a run, while if you hook a fish on the tail fly you can, if you are careful, play the fish with the dropper out of the water most of the time. A far bigger risk in my opinion is another salmon taking the dropper while you are playing the fish, I have seen this happen several times and inevitably it ends in disaster as the fish usually swim in different directions although twice I have seen both landed.

Personally I never change my dropper and content myself with ringing the changes on my tail fly. To show how effective the dropper can be and to show how strange salmon fishing can be even at its best I will tell you the following story. I was once asked to fish a neighbouring river as a guest and I arrived in the morning with my rod up and a dropper on my cast which happened to be a small Hairy Mary. The ghillie who met me viewed the dropper with disapproval, said that the river was far too rocky to use a dropper and suggested that I took it off. However I refused. At lunch I had caught six fish, all on the dropper, and even though I had changed my tail fly several times I had not had a single offer to it. The ghillie remained unconvinced that the dropper had anything to do with my success and said that it was just that particular pattern of fly which was effective that day. So I gave him my fly box and told him to put an exact replica of the successful Hairy Mary on the tail. This he did, but the upshot of this extraordinary story was that by the evening I had caught a further seven salmon, all of them on the dropper, and I can't remember moving a salmon to the tail fly all day. Thereafter that ghillie always insisted that all the fishermen he accompanied used a dropper when the water temperature rose above 45°F and needless to say it was always the Hairy Mary that he chose!

As summer advances and the water temperatures rise to the late 50°'s and 60°'s F salmon become more lethargic and generally move far more shyly and slowly when taking a fly. You should therefore fish your fly as slowly as possible to give the fish ample time to size it up before they take it. This should be done by altering the angle of your cast making the cast more downstream than across and where this is not possible mending your line continually so that the fly traverses the river as slowly as possible. If you handline then you should cut down the length of line that you pull in and work your fly extremely slowly. I hardly ever draw in more than two inches at a time until I get to the end of the cast when I pull in more line to make sure that the fly is buoyant before casting again. Fishing in this way I am constantly in touch with my fly and I can therefore strike instantaneously whenever I feel a fish.

It is important to realise what you are doing when you fish in this way. Anyone who moves his fly in this way and remains constantly in direct contact is in effect imitating a small invertebrate or fish, swimming against the current. Wood, the great inventor of greased line fishing for salmon, advocated keeping the fly as still in the water as possible, and mending the line to avoid drag. By this means his fly hung motionless in the water. By doing this he was in effect imitating plankton one of the salmon's staple foods in the sea and there is no doubt that this can be an effective way of presenting your fly in the summer, and it can kill fish freely when all other methods have failed. However when you do this it is inevitable that you are seldom if ever in direct contact with your fly, and therefore when you move a fish you should follow Wood's advice and give the fish line when you see the boil or your line start to draw away from you.

In my long experience served on the banks of many rivers I have seen many interesting things and not the least interesting has been the many strange objects that a salmon will sometimes take. I have seen salmon rise to cigarette ends, wood chippings, leaves on many occasions and crusts of bread, all of which were immediately rejected. On one occasion I saw a large salmon in the Major Pool on the Welsh Dee rise to and take eleven different leaves in a short space of time. I was fishing with a floating prawn at the time which I took off and putting on a leaf tried to become the first recorded salmon fisher to catch a salmon on a leaf. However although the fish moved deep several times when I floated the leaf over him he did not take it, and I imagine the drag of the line put him off. On another occasion in the narrow section of a long flat pool in the north of Scotland I saw a salmon rise to a succession of mayflies which floated over him. As it was Sunday I spent an amusing hour collecting mayflies and floating them over him. He took about two-thirds of those which I put in his way and the ones he did not take were those which I had damaged in handling. I know that salmon have been caught on mayflies on the Test and it would have been interesting to see whether this one could have been caught in the same way.

I have also seen salmon rise at the knot which joins line and cast and on more than one occasion I have felt the pull as the fish closed his mouth. They will also take spinning weights. Just after the war a firm of tackle makers produced red spinning weights which were an infernal nuisance as the fish were always taking them and after several pulls without any connection I could plainly see the marks of the salmon's teeth on the lead.

Few people realise the speed and accuracy of the salmon's movement in the water and the superb judgement of the fish when he takes a lure. Prawn fishers who have mounted their prawns without sufficient care will know that a salmon will take the head off the prawn without touching the hook. For the benefit of those who do not fish the prawn, I must explain that for all three methods, spinning, floating and sink and draw, the prawn is mounted so that the hooks are embedded in the head. And for the rambling or floating prawn the hook is embedded in the head using a bait needle to thread the gut through the body of the crustacean. When one thinks of the speed with which a prawn is travelling in the water such accuracy seems incredible.

Another thing that many people do not realise is that salmon invariably go for the head of the fly. When the long tailed streamer flies first appeared many anglers hesitated to use them because they felt that the salmon would just touch the tail of the fly which in many cases overlapped the hook by as much as two inches. In practice this happens very rarely and the long tailed flies have a successful hooking rate. I also think that they are successful lures because the tail moves in a life-like manner in the water far more so than the traditional fly.

But I am digressing from my subject which is summer fishing. If you find that the conditions are poor and that you are achieving no success fishing in the normal manner, don't despair for there are several different ways of presenting your fly to the fish which are well worth trying. The first of these is known as 'dibbling'. For this you mount two flies on your cast, generally a double-hooked fly size 5 or smaller on the dropper and a larger or heavier fly on the tail. The object is to bounce the dropper along the top of the water in the fast streamy runs at the head of each pool. It is rather like the old-fashioned method of loch fishing, of working the fly so that the dropper was half out of the water.

For anyone who has not fished in this way I will describe the procedure.

To start with you should get as close to the run as you can and if you have to wade you should take care to move as quietly and carefully as possible. Then starting right at the top of the run cast a short line pretty square across the current. When you have made the cast raise the top of your rod to bring the dropper to the top of the water and then try to bounce it as slowly as you can across the stream. It is a good idea to make three or four casts from each position and you should pay particular attention to the quiet corners behind rocks and to the slacker water just on either side of the fast current. Try to hang your fly in the current over any places like this in the run and then let the current swing the fly away. Very often the fish will take just as the fly moves away. I generally move down two yards at a time and make several casts to make sure I have explored all the water thoroughly. If you have to cast a longer line than you can control with the top of the rod then you can sometimes get the fly to work by handlining. Fishing a stream in this way does take longer than fishing it in the normal way but there is only a short stretch of water where there is enough current to allow you to do this and when you reach the end of the fast water you can fish out the rest of the pool in the normal way.

Dibbling is a most interesting method of fishing and part of its fascination is that, unless you are engaged in deep conversation with someone standing behind you, you will inevitably see the fish take and it is amazing how close to you they will rise to the fly. Fish coming to the fly fished in this way generally come in three different ways. They either move very quietly to it and seem to suck the fly off the surface. Alternatively they make a beautiful head and tail rise to the fly and take it down as they submerge. Thirdly many fish dash at the fly in a very violent manner making a tremendous wallop on the water. I think that fish coming to the fly like this are trying to drown it and I find that they tend to miss the fly altogether. Indeed you will find that fishing in this way you may move many more fish than you will hook. When you do rise a fish it is imperative that you give it time to take the fly either by dropping the point of your rod or by giving the fish line. Dropping the point of the rod is generally easier and quicker. If you don't do this you will find that you generally just prick the fish. Dibbling can work well on bright days in very low water and you can use this method in very small streams or pots which cannot be fished in any other manner.

As to the flies you can use anglers who are experienced in the method of fishing will have their own favourites. I have found a blonde Hairy

Mary, the Sweep, Monro Killer or Stoat's Tail very effective. And the Munro Killer with its long tail is particularly good in high water conditions. Personally I use double-hooked flies, but many fishermen prefer trebles. The disadvantage of trebles is that they tend to get tangled up with the main leader, and this happens most frequently when there is a high wind. In very strong winds it is difficult to fish in this way. Don't have too long a leg to your dropper, 2–3 inches is ample and don't have the dropper attachment too far up the cast away from the tail fly. If you find that the dropper is not behaving correctly this is probably the reason or else your tail fly is not heavy enough to anchor the dropper properly.

The river where this method of fishing is most practised is the Helmsdale, which with its many runs and small streamy pools is ideally suited to this method of fishing. Here it was that Major Gilroy one of the greatest exponents of the art made this method of fishing so popular. But there are many other rivers where it can be and is practised successfully.

A variation of dibbling is just to fish with one large tube fly on the tail. Use a tube fly of between 1–3 inches in length according to the conditions, and when you have made your cast bring the tube to the surface so that the treble at the end of the tube is bouncing along the surface then let it submerge again and repeat the performance. Using a large tube works best in very fast water and it is better to fish with a longish rod, if you have a choice, but if you are faced with a stream which you cannot reach with a short line you can fish a large tube using the sink and draw method to bring the fly spluttering to the surface. If you are using a single tube I think it is best to use one that is pretty heavily dressed, which will make a pronounced wake on the water. Fished in this way it imitates a creature in distress or one that is trying to escape and on many occasions it has saved a blank day.

One of the greatest artists of this method of fishing was the late Willie Duncan, a keeper for many years at Skelpick Lodge in Strath Naver. He used to fish like this on the Naver with great success and seldom failed to move a fish even under the most unpromising conditions. This particular method can often move fish that are lying very deep, and provided there is enough current it can take fish from areas of pools that are quite unproductive fished in any other way.

Once again fish who take the dragged tube either do so very quietly, and if they do you must give them line, or very fast and voraciously often making a tremendous splash on top of the fly. If they do this you really

94

can't do very much about it for you won't have time and they are either hooked solidly or not at all.

The last variation is to fish with what the Americans would call a 'riffling hitch'. To work this you have to fish with a floating line and use a tube fly. Put a half-hitch round the body of the tube or pierce a hole half-way down the body of the tube and insert your gut through this hole instead of the eye of the tube. If you pull the fly gently against the current it will cock up in a crabwise fashion and drag across the surface imitating a drowning creature or one that is in distress. The great advantage of using the riffling hitch is that it can be fished over a wide area of water and you are not confined to the streamy parts of the river. The size of the tube depends on the height of water and the nature of the pool but generally a tube from ½–1½ inches is best.

The last resort is to fish with a dry fly. Dry fly fishing for salmon has never been very successful over here, although it is an accepted way of catching fish in America. Possibly the reason is that the water temperature seldom rises into the middle to high 60°F which present the best conditions. While there are people who regularly fish with the dry fly and achieve a measure of success I think the real reason why it is not practised more often is that people only use the dry fly as the last resort when conditions are totally hopeless and if it was used more often in reasonable fishing conditions it would prove more effective. Another reason is that you have to be prepared to persevere fishing over one fish for a long time. Constant casting seems to irritate the salmon who are then goaded into taking. If you do want to try it the best fly patterns are some of those developed for the American market, the Rat-faced Macdougall, Grey Wulff and White Wulff being the best known.

In my opinion any of these methods of presenting the fly to the salmon are well worth trying in the summer months. I would go further and say that the reason why they are not practised more is that people who have read about them, or been told of them only try them as a last resort, and when they fail discard them as useless. The dry fly is probably the best example of this.

If two people are sharing a beat it can often pay for one angler to fish with one method, and the other another. Very often the fish which will not respond to the fly presented in the traditional manner, will accept a dragged tube or the fly fished with a riffling hitch and if on any day one method appears to be moving more fish than the other then both anglers can resort to it. I think that it is interesting that most of these variations have been perfected in the North of Scotland where on the majority of rivers fly only is the rule. Elsewhere when conditions are unfavourable for fly fishing anglers resort to spinning or bait fishing. One of the advantages of fishing with the fly is that you only need one rod and you can change from one method to another in a matter of minutes. If you have to carry two rods and a plethora of minnows, prawns, etc., you will waste valuable fishing time and can end up by not persevering long enough with any one method to give it a chance to be successful.

Autumn Fishing

When I say autumn fishing I am taking the 1st September as my starting date, which can, of course, be a pretty arbitrary decision; particularly if we happen to have a long hot summer which goes on well into that month. But there are reasons for that date. First of all many rivers in the British Isles close their seasons at the end of that month. Some continue until the 15th October and others until the 31st October, with the single exception of the Tweed which closes on the 30th November. So in the salmon fisher's calendar there are generally only a few weeks left of the year. Secondly, in spite of exceptions the weather begins to change, the nights draw in and become colder, often in the Highlands there is a nip of frost in the air and this all changes the character of the fishing and the methods and techniques that you should use. So for me autumn fishing starts on the 1st September.

Really autumn fishing can and should be split into two categories. The first is the river which has a genuine run of fresh fish coming into the system and the Tweed is much the best known example of this type of river. The second is where there is no genuine autumn run of fish as such, but any river where large catches are made either of fish which have been in the river for some time, or where fish that have been in the estuary move into the bottom reaches of the river before spawning and the reason why so many fish are caught at this time of the year lies in the change of the seasons. As I have said many times before the main reason why conditions are good is the air/water temperature gap.

As the nights lengthen and grow colder the water temperature will start to drop rapidly and also the peat stain that is so common in Highland rivers in the summer will start to disappear. There is there-fore a much better chance of the angler finding the water/air temperature gap in his favour and a further factor is that the salmon will now respond to a much larger variety of fly sizes and fishing techniques than they will in summerlike conditions. And it can even be profitable, in high water, to return to the sunk line and large fly tactics of the spring.

To start with let me deal with those rivers which are due to close at the end of September or early October. Generally the main stock of fish is to be found in the upper reaches of those rivers where the salmon have congregated near their spawning beds, either in the tributaries or the main river. At this time of the year the fish will tend to lie, not in the big holding pools of the spring but in the streams and slower moving gravelly pools, either pools in which they will spawn or pools that give a ready access to the spawning grounds. The only exception is when the main run of fish have been held back for many months by abnormally dry weather conditions, and if that is the case then the whole river system will be a hive of activity as the fish move upstream to get to their spawning grounds. It is worth noting that on some of the shorter Highland rivers which have formidable falls some-where in their length, such a drought can be tremendously damaging, for gravid fish cannot negotiate these obstacles with the same ease as when they are fresh run into the river in the summer and they then have no alternative but to fall back and use the spawning grounds below these obstacles. In many cases such spawning grounds may be severely limited, and become very overcrowded, which results in a serious loss of spawning stock. While at other times the water level may be so low in the spawning season that a large part of the spawning stock of a burn or tributary may be unable to enter it in the spawning season.

On rivers that have a genuine autumn run then the whole river can fish well, even the bottom beats can be very productive while the higher up the river you go the more you will begin to overlap with the earlier spring and summer runs of fish. There can be some difficulty here because in order to cull this late run of fish the whole river system must be kept open which can well result in a large number of gravid hen fish being caught with a resulting loss to the spawning stock in the river. Some proprietors have a rule that all dark hen fish caught at this time of the year must be returned to the water. Whether many survive capture and release, I rather doubt, but if this rule is in force then I feel it should be accompanied by one limiting the angler to the use of single hooked flies which are far easier to unhook than double-hooked flies or triangles which can get so embedded that they have to be almost cut out. If this happens I very much doubt whether the salmon survives. A gravid hen fish, caught at this time of the year, is in any case poor eating.

It is interesting that very often the average weight of the fish killed at this time of year is often far higher than at any other. Many of the dark cock fish caught weigh between 12 and 20 lbs and many of the fresh run fish straight out of the sea also weigh from 12–20 lbs. So this does add to the challenge. And a further challenge is that fish often play very much harder than they do at any other time of the year.

Fishing in the early autumn up to the end of September often varies little from the summer months. But as the water temperature drops a far wider selection of fly sizes can be used and it often pays the angler to carry both floating and sunk lines and try a sunk line if he has had no success with a floater. If the water is clear and the river is not running very high then start off fishing with a fly size 8 or 9 but do not hesitate to put on a much larger fly up to a 1/0 or size 1 if these prove ineffective. If you are lucky enough to have high water then there is nothing to stop you fishing with a sunk line and a 2½ inch tube as you would in the spring and such tactics can often be very successful.

I think that it is very important to take the temperature of the water very carefully at this time of year, for often even in late autumn if the weather has been mild you will find the water temperature well above 42° even in a high river. If this happens you are much more likely to be successful with a floating line and a small size of fly and I have known occasions when the only successful angler was using these tactics when all the others were fishing with large tubes and sunk lines. There is no doubt that when the water temperature lies in the range of 42°–50°F salmon can be caught on a large number of flies in various different sizes and you must be prepared to ring the changes and experiment until you find a size of fly that the fish will take.

There are two drawbacks to fishing in the autumn apart from the quality of the catch. The first of these is that cock fish develop that hook in their lower jaw, known as a kipe, which often grows so large that it makes it difficult for him to close his mouth completely. Often when a cock fish takes a fly at this time of the year there is a gap of 1–2 inches between the top and bottom jaws through which the fly can be drawn, and unless he is hooked firmly in the scissors, many a cock fish, at this time of the year, will just be pricked or lightly hooked and lost. This is one reason I feel why the majority of fish caught at this time of the year are hens.

Another major disadvantage on wooded stretches of rivers, particularly if you have a high wind, rain or a rising river, conditions hopeless enough in themselves, is leaf fall. On rivers that are heavily wooded the fisherman is continually catching leaves and also I feel that the fish get tired of seeing an endless succession of objects floating over their heads. In my opinion in these conditions much the best thing for the angler to do is to put on a slow sinking line and fish a weighted fly low in the water. That is if you want to keep on casting, if you don't you can go home.

Tidal Freshwater Estuaries

Tidal freshwater estuaries are not all that common but they do occur and as I have one on my doorstep, I will describe it and say how it is fished so that anyone who has the chance of fishing this type of water can tackle it in the best way. The Kyle of Sutherland, near where I live, is nearly 19 miles long: from its exit to the sea at the Dornoch Firth up to the Invershin Hotel is 11 miles; while from the Invershin Hotel up to the junction of the Cassley and Oykel is a further 8 miles. The lower stretch is affected by the influx of salt water but above the Invershin Hotel the Kyle is freshwater and the rise and fall is caused by the tide backing up the freshwater outflow. At the top where the two rivers join the tidal effect at neap tides is between one and two feet depending on the flow of the rivers while at spring tides the tidal effect is three feet at low water flows.

Salmon fishing by any means in any water touched by the salt water of the seas is not very effective. Sea trout can be caught, indeed sea trout can be freely taken in the sea itself, but salmon just don't take. Where the tide, as in the Kyle of Sutherland, just backs up the freshwater, salmon can be caught, and sometimes they take the fly quite freely.

All these long estuary stretches are inevitably very slow and sluggish and except in very high water conditions there will be insufficient current to work the fly so the first requisite is a wind to ruffle the surface of the water. Given a wind they can be fished either from the bank or from a boat in exactly the same way as a loch.

The best time to fish is during a period of prolonged drought. In a long estuary like the Kyle of Sutherland fish will come into the estuary and often they rest there in considerable numbers waiting for the pull of the freshwater to bring them up into their rivers. Nevertheless in any estuary where fish do pause to rest there is always the chance of finding a fish whatever the water conditions.

What conditions do you look for and when should you fish? In nearly all cases, except in extreme low water conditions, you need a wind blowing down river in the same direction as the ebb tide. Then if you are fishing from a boat you can get a long drift downstream over the fishable water at a reasonable speed. A wind blowing upstream against the ebb tide will, of course, produce a better ripple but unless the river flow is very, very low and the wind very strong, the combined currents of the ebb flow and the land water coming down will create too strong a current for the boat to drift against.

However in very low water conditions a good upstream wind will be enough to make the boat drift against the ebb tide and these conditions can be good.

You can, of course, fish from the bank, and where the combination of tide and wind make it unsuitable to work the boat properly then this is probably the best thing to do.

Now it is a fact, why I don't know, that you will not catch a salmon or a grilse on the fly when the tide is flowing. Even when you have a wind blowing upstream with the tide creating ideal angling conditions you will catch nothing. In forty years of fishing the Kyle of Sutherland I have never caught a salmon or seen a salmon caught on the main period of the flow tide after the first half hour after the tide has turned. Although funnily enough this does not apply to worm fishing, where the opposite seems to be the case. A local worthy I know, used to get beautiful baskets of sea trout and even the odd salmon worming on the flow tide but he told me he never had much success when the tide was ebbing. So the first thing you must do is to study the local tide tables and plan to fish on the ebb tide and say 45 minutes on either side of it to coincide with the 'turn of the tide'. Indeed it is the half an hour on the turn of the tide that promises the best chance of success.

For salmon and grilse the rougher the day the better, and except for the period at the turn of the tide, they hardly ever take at all freely in less than a 3 inch wave. The best days of all are when there are white horses and troughs between the waves and it is tremendously exciting then seeing the dark shape of the salmon come up in between the waters to seize the fly.

I have often noticed that fish are far moodier in an estuary than they normally are in a river. Sometimes you can move up to 20 fish on a tide without one taking hold of your fly while on other occasions you will just move one or two fish but they will take solidly. I have also many, many times fished a whole tide in seemingly perfect conditions when I knew that there were plenty of fish about and never had an offer, but at times like these if you fish on till the turn of the tide you are generally assured of moving one or two fish or even more. But as the taking period is so short often if you hook a good fish by the time you have landed him the taking period is over.

If you are in a boat during the turn of the tide and fishing two rods, each rod is quite likely to hook a fish at the same instant, and then, unless you have an experienced boatman, the fun really begins. It is pretty essential for one of the rods to lead their fish round to the other side of the boat which reduces the chance of the lines becoming entangled.

In tidal stretches fish often seem to congregate round a burn mouth. There is little doubt that some of these fish will never pass this point, and at spawning time will enter the burn to spawn. Others are natives of the bigger rivers and are only awaiting more favourable conditions to continue their journeys upstream. Anyone fishing these reaches should pay particular attention to any place where a large burn comes in.

During the early part of the season when water temperatures are under 45°F, it is best to use tube flies from 1–2 inches in length or if you are using ordinary flies, sizes 1–3. If you are fishing from a boat a 12 foot rod is ideal and you should cast a moderate length of line, but at this time of year the water flows are likely to be high and you may well be better to fish from the bank. A 14 foot rod should enable you to cover most of the best lies and if I were you I would back the water up.

Once the water temperature rises above 45°F you are, I think, best to use sea trout flies size 8 in all conditions, although if conditions are very bright with very low water flow and little wind you can fish smaller. If you fear that the hooks of these small flies may not be strong enough then you can fish with very small tube flies or lightly dressed low water salmon flies.

You may well find as summer progresses that weed growth will prevent you covering the water adequately if you are fishing from the bank. If this is the case you just have to look for places where you can cast. Very often there will be narrow stretches where the estuary deepens and in such places you can often fish the ebb tide as you would a pool on a river. Otherwise you should back the water up. You won't be able, generally, to fish your bob fly on the surface unless there is the odd high promontory to enable you to do this, so just fish an ordinary sunk fly on a floating line. Have three flies on your cast if you can because if there are sea trout around, and there generally will be, this will offer them a wider selection, but if the wind is very awkward and casting difficult you are probably better off just with one.

In the summer when fishing from a boat, I use a sea trout rod and a cast of three sea trout flies. Salmon take these just as readily as any other pattern. The ones I favour are a Black Pennel, Soldier Palmer or Badger on the bob, a Grouse and Claret, Teal and Green or Silver Butcher in the centre, and an Invicta or Peter Ross on the tail. In very rough conditions I have seen a big Loch Ordie fly work well in the bob position, and a fairly large size worm fly do well on the tail. If you do want to mount a tube fly my advice is to put it in the tail position as otherwise the treble can get tangled in the cast which is irritating. Either cast a fairly long line and then handline your flies back towards you, fishing fairly deep, or else use the old fashioned Scottish method of loch fishing of casting a shorter line and then immediately bringing your bob fly to the surface as soon as your cast lands on the water. This method can be very effective, particularly in the warm days of summer when water conditions are low. I find it a most exciting method of fishing especially when you see a salmon or sea trout take the bob fly off the surface either with a head and tail rise or a big swirl as he sucks it in. Then in the words of William Caine 'oh my brother, oh my learned brother, do not strike too soon . . .' You really do have to restrain yourself and delay a few seconds before striking, and even if you do not touch the fish it is surprising how often he will come again the next cast.

If you are fishing your bob fly on the surface then any fish taking the middle or tail fly will make a boil as they take and a salmon or grilse must be given time before you strike. Sea trout on the other hand take much more quickly than salmon and you should tighten straight away. And of course the result of this is that you will be too quick for the salmon and too slow for the sea trout. Really only experience of fishing this type of water where both species of fish are present will teach you to distinguish between them as they take the fly. The only tips that I can give you are that salmon and grilse are generally bigger so that they displace more water, i.e. make a bigger boil when they come to the fly and sea trout generally seem to be moving more quickly and very often splash at the fly. But in time you will develop a sixth sense about this.

If you are fishing a long line and your flies are below the surface then, unless the fish comes to you right at the end of your cast, you will generally feel the fish before you see the boil, and therefore you are less likely to mistime your strike.

Perhaps it is worth noting that the lower reaches of many rivers are influenced by the tide whether the salt water penetrates into the river mouth or not. If the tide just backs up the fresh water then, particularly in low water conditions fishing is improved when the tide starts to ebb as the outflow naturally increases. This is a help to both the salmon and sea trout angler. If the salt water penetrates into the river then only the sea trout fisher benefits. But as a corollary once the tide starts to flow the angler's chance of success is much reduced.

Loch Fishing

Loch fishing for salmon has much in common with my preceding chapter. There are many lochs in Scotland where good sport can be obtained fly fishing for salmon, particularly on the north and west coasts and in the islands off the west coast. And in many cases these lochs are connected with the sea, by very short rivers with no falls to impede the passage of the fish, and so in many cases, salmon grilse and sea trout will arrive in the loch, fresh and with sea lice on them and for this reason they can take the fly very readily. Fresh water lochs are not, of course, affected by the tide and so they can fish well all day, and the only essential for good salmon fishing is that there is a good wave. Indeed it would be fair to say that the rougher the day the better; and conditions with a gentle breeze and a 1–3 inch ripple, ideal for sea trout fishing, are not nearly so good for salmon fishing.

As in all forms of fishing, local knowledge is almost an essential, and it is probably more important in a loch than on a river. Salmon take best in shallow water up to 8 feet in depth. They are rarely taken in deep water on a fly and therefore it is imperative that you know the nature of the bed and depth of your loch. Most lochs apart from having shallow bays and shallow areas around a lot of the shore, have rocky shingly banks further off shore where you will find salmon lying and therefore it is the greatest help if you have a ghillie who knows where such places are for there is your best chance of sport. When very strong winds are blowing on shore then salmon can be caught right in the very shallows, where they will lie with their tails literally touching the gravel. It is obvious that to have any chance of catching these fish you must have rough conditions as otherwise the salmon will see the approaching boat and be disturbed by the movement of the rod. If conditions are right you can very often get fish coming to the fly as

Fishing on a windy day, Loch Ailsh

close to the boat as the point of the oar but at other times all you will see is a deep boil as the fish turns away, scared by what he has seen.

Remember that the water of these lochs is usually gin clear and on a bright clear day you can see right down into the depths.

One of the troubles with salmon fishing on a loch is that on the best days it is really only possible to have one angler in the boat. Then the boatman can hold the boat's head into the wind and work his way along the shore which allows the angler to fish the water to the best advantage. If there are two anglers in the boat the boatman perforce has to drift broadside with the wind and very often the boat will drift too quickly for the anglers to cover the water properly. Perhaps I should say that if you do hook a fish it is a good idea to lead it away from the shore so that the taking area is as little disturbed as possible.

Always make sure that you fish the areas near the mouth of any burn very thoroughly. Salmon who will ascend the burns to spawn later in the year will often lie off the mouth and when the burns are in spate, or the right wind conditions prevail, you can often get tremendous sport.

The lochs at the head of the short west coast rivers have always been famed for their sea trout fishing and their potential as salmon lochs was largely ignored until recently when sea trout stocks have declined so drastically mainly because of UDN. There is no doubt that fishing on these lochs for the west coast sea trout which would frequently run to 8 lbs with the outside chance of catching a fish of up to 18 lbs, was tremendously attractive but as I have said it is really a different technique from loch fishing for salmon. You require different conditions for success and nowadays you see more boats hugging the shoreline, rather than drifting the deeper parts of the loch trying to tempt the sea trout from their depths. Dapping, one of the most attractive forms of all fishing, is not really as effective for salmon as it is for sea trout, and I would surmise that the sale of floss silk lines has dropped.

As for tackle I think that you do not require anything other than a normal sea trout or trout rod and you can use either a floating or slow sinking line. The only thing I think you should have is a reel that is large enough to take at least 100 yards of backing for if a salmon decides to go then it can go a long way very quickly. If you are fishing a slow sinking line cast a fairly long line and allow your flies to sink reasonably deeply, this is probably most effective on cold days, days with a lightish wind or conversely days when the wind is so high that you cannot control the fly properly on the surface.

Alternatively, fish with a floating line and drag the bob fly on the surface. On warm days with a steady wind this is probably the best method to pursue.

In lochs which contain both salmon and sea trout you will have the same difficulty in distinguishing between the takes of the two species as I outlined in the chapter on *Freshwater Estuaries*. Only experience will guide you and the only additional point I would make is that in lochs, salmon sometimes follow the fly right into the boat and then take almost as the fly leaves the water.

Once a fish is hooked it can behave in a sulky fashion boring deeply and often trying to get under the boat, there is always the danger then that one of the loose flies will catch if this happens and a good man at the oars is essential so that he can turn the boat quickly and prevent this. Otherwise the fish may take off often ending a long run with a jump. Once the fish is under control then the boatman can lead it around the loch in exactly the same way as you can walk a fish up in a pool and sometimes it can pay dividends for the boatman to row ashore and the angler finish the battle from the stem of the boat. The reason for this is that a sulky fish can often take a long time to kill in deep water particularly if it is being played on a light rod and if it is led into shallower water and then played from the shore it can shorten the battle. And finally do, if you have three flies on your cast, play it right out before you attempt to net it otherwise there is the risk that one of the flies will catch on the net before the fish is in it with disastrous results.

As to flies I think that you will do best by just using normal sea trout patterns. If you wish you can fish a small tube fly such as a Stoat's Tail, Hairy Mary or Shrimp fly on the tail, and these are just as effective for sea trout as they are for salmon; if I am fishing a Stoat's Tail I prefer to use a silver treble to give the fly some relief and these small silver trebles can be used with any pattern of tube fly with equal effect. Of the sea trout flies I have had most success for salmon with either an Invicta, Greenwell or Grouse and Claret, all of which can be fished either on the tail or the centre but there are many other of the sea trout patterns which can be equally good. On the bob there are a fairly wide variety from which to choose but a Black Pennel is by far my favourite and in rough conditions a Loch Ordie can be very effective. I have seen a Muddler's Minnow used with great effect by several of my friends but once again conditions must be on the rough side for this to have any real effect. There is nothing to prevent you using any of the authentic low water salmon flies, size 8–10 being large enough for any purpose and again these can also be just as effective for sea trout.

Occasionally you catch salmon when you are side casting as you row between drifts but I have never seen this method be really effective except on occasions when with one angler in the boat the ghillie is rowing very slowly along a shoreline. You can also catch the odd fish trolling the three flies on a long line behind a boat.

It is an advantage especially on the calmer days, to use a fairly long cast of fine nylon. A cast of 6–10 lbs breaking strain is perfectly adequate, but on windy rough days you can well afford to fish nylon up to 12–16 lbs if you desire.

Fishing on lochs can sometimes be very frustrating because as many of them are sited amongst high mountain ranges some directions of wind do not suit the lie of the loch and therefore, on many occasions you may be becalmed and have to while away a long tedious day amid beautiful scenery but often plagued by a hoard of midges. On other occasions you can find yourself chasing a fluky wind round the loch with little chance of success. Often even after a decent wind does get up it is unusual to have much success for the first half hour period after the wind becomes constant. If it is varying from different directions then again these conditions do not seem to suit good angling.

On other occasions because of the steep mountains surrounding some of these lochs, a high wind from the wrong direction can often buffet off the steep mountain sides causing treacherous conditions commonly known as 'spin drift' which makes holding a boat both hazardous and even dangerous at times and in a gale can easily prevent the boats either getting out at all or confine them to a very small sheltered area of the loch.

In very hot dry summers the fish that would have entered the loch may well be held back in the estuary by lack of water and also the banks and shallow areas that are normally the most productive places, become too shallow to fish. You are then forced to fish deeper parts of the loch which are practically useless for wet fly fishing. In these conditions I would dap using a longer rod and a single dapping fly blown out on a silk floss line provided there is enough wind to allow the dapping line to work. This method of fishing can be highly exciting and very effective for sea trout but it is as I have said not nearly so effective for salmon but it is certainly possible to take the odd fish on occasions.

You really do have to steel yourself with all the will power you can command not to strike too quickly, when the fish comes to the dap, but to give both sea trout and salmon plenty of time to take the dap fly down below the surface of the water before raising your rod.

Anyone fishing one of the west coast lochs nestled amongst what is very often breathtaking mountain scenery, has, not only the scenery, but also many types of bird, animal and insect life to distract his concentration at the wrong moment of the day – which is yet another hazard against the angler and in favour of the quarry!

The Life Cycle of a Salmon

Salmon are born and bred in fresh water, mainly in the headwaters of our river systems or its tributaries. The female or hen salmon first of all cuts a trench in the gravel of the river bed by turning on her side and forcing the water down onto the river bed. When the gravel is displaced from the river bed it is essential that there is sufficient current flowing over the bed to wash it downstream, otherwise the gravel will just fall back into place. This is part of the reason why successful spawning in still water is practically impossible except when wind wave action replaces the effect of water flow. A surface flow of 12–18 inches per second is considered the most favourable condition but it must not be less than 3 inches per second. Having made an indent in the gravel the female then perfects her trench by use of her ventral fins, body and point of her tail. The trench will now be 6–9 inches and in the bottom of it she will have positioned two stones between which she will deposit her eggs. When she is ready to spawn she takes up what is known as the crouch position in the trench and opens her mouth whereupon she is immediately joined by the male who comes alongside her. Both fish then extrude eggs and sperm simultaneously. The female normally ejects approximately 2000 eggs into each depression. An 8 lb salmon will produce about 800 eggs per pound of body weight and a 5 lb grilse about 500 eggs per pound of body weight.

The hen fish then cuts another depression above the first one and the gravel displaced from the second depression will fill the first one. Generally a hen fish will cut 3 or 4 depressions and finally she will cut a blind depression to displace enough gravel to cover her last lot of eggs. The area of gravel within which the eggs are deposited is known as a redd. When they have spawned both the adult salmon will drop

SEA

In the sea they
feed voraciously

Smolt migrates to sea
at 4-6 inches in
length in April-June.

Smolt

Early Grilse
(about 2-3 lbs)

After 1-5 years
the Parr assumes
a silver coat and
moves downstream.

Later Grilse
(about 5-6
lbs - some
are heavier)

Parr

Fish stop
feeding on
return to fresh
water.

Grilse
return to
the river
after one
sea winter.

Salmon returns to
the river after two
or more sea winters
(from about 6 lbs
upwards).

After about
6 months the
young fish is
known as a
Parr.

R I V E R

Fry

As Autumn approaches
the fish develop eggs
and milt,   and
darken in   colour

Grilse and
Salmon spawn
November to January.

The eggs hatch
after 12-20 weeks.

Alevin has
yolk sac attached,
they emerge from
the gravel after
3-4 weeks.

After spawning the
fish regain their
silver colour and are
known as kelts. Many
die, a few return to the
sea and come back to
spawn again.

(Not to Scale)

downstream exhausted. Over 90% of males die immediately after spawning and few survive to return to the sea, but about 40% of hen fish return to the sea and just under half of these will return to the river to spawn a second time. It is however rare to find a male spawning a second time. Salmon spawn between the end of October and early February, with the vast majority spawning in November and December.

In passing perhaps I should say that an adequate supply of good spawning gravel is the single most important thing for a salmon river to possess. This gravel must be clean, easily workable, open to allow free percolation of water, and finally it must be stable otherwise if it moves for instance in a flood the ova will be washed away before it incubates.

After fertilisation the ova will incubate and the period of incubation depends entirely on the mean water temperature. At 45°F the eggs will hatch in approximately 84 days but at 37°F the eggs will take approximately 145 days to hatch. This is a marvellous example of the provision of nature, for only when the water temperature rises to 40°F will there be enough food available for the fry to live on when they hatch and this will vary not only throughout the country but at different altitudes in the catchment area of any one river.

When the egg is first planted it is extremely fragile and can be ruptured very easily in which case it dies immediately. The movement of gravel caused by another fish cutting a redd on top of the gravel that the ova lies in can be quite sufficient to either kill them, expose them, or bury them too deep for them to survive. However after approximately half of the mean incubation period, the ova become eyed, and the casing of the egg hardens. After this stage they can be handled quite freely with little damage and it is common practice to move the eggs from the hatchery at this stage and plant them out in river systems either in vibert boxes which are placed in the gravel or in artificial redds specially constructed. Large quantities of eggs from hatcheries are also sold at this stage and can be transported large distances without fear of damage.

When the ova hatches it then becomes known as an aelvin. An aelvin is a little, almost transparent creature, under an inch in length which has a yolk sac hanging under its gills. This yolk sac provides food for the aelvin as it works its way up through the gravel onto the surface of the river bed. During this journey it meets its first predator the stone fly larva which pierces the yolk sac and the aelvin then dies of starvation, and when it gets to the surface of the river bed it meets the eel which is another predator. Once they arrive at the surface of the riverbed and the yolk sac is completely absorbed they become known as fry and spread out in their new environment to look for food to sustain themselves. At first they do not move far and use the cover of pebbles and larger stones not only to protect them from the force of the current but also to shield them from the many predators that lurk in the deeper water, these are numerous and vary from numerous larger fish of different species to many birds the best known of which are the cormorant, heron, merganser, goosander, all the varied gulls and lastly, some say, that attractive little bird, the dipper.

As these little fish get used to their new environment and gain in strength and size from feeding on waterborne insects, invertebrates and fresh water plankton, they begin to take up their own feeding territory using all the shallow areas and keeping away from fast currents which would wash them down into deeper water where they would almost inevitably be devoured. Losses at this stage and in the previous stage are extremely high in spite of, on average, an extremely high hatch rate which is something like 97.5%. It is normally acknowledged that approximately 96% of those that hatch will die in their first six months but after six months young salmon are far more able to look after themselves and often establish predominance on their nursery area. At this stage they are known as parr. The growth rate of the little fish entirely depends on two things, firstly the amount of feed available in the river system and secondly the length of feeding period they are allowed per annum. This is once again entirely controlled by water temperature as they remain dormant and barely feed at all when water temperatures are under 42°F therefore, the duration of the feeding period varies tremendously throughout the country and throughout the catchment area. In mild seasons and especially mild winters they could be able to feed for all except about ten weeks whereas in severe weather conditions and in countries such as Norway the feeding period could be limited to as little as 5–6 months.

The parr's main dangers are from the bigger predators, both fish and bird and also the careless angler. In the latter case with the limited food supply of the river system the trout fisher's worm or fly is a very tasty morsel to the poor uneducated creature and many are caught. In some cases the angler recognises what he has caught and releases them immediately but unfortunately if they are hooked badly and are bleeding when they are released they will not survive, in other cases entirely through ignorance the trout fisher does not realise what he has caught and puts them in his creel, this is especially common when children are fishing.

Once a parr has reached 4–6 inches in length the urge of migration becomes strong and during the months of March to June the larger parr put on a silver livery and begin their seaward migration. At this stage they are known as smolts. The age that they migrate varies enormously. It depends once again on the feeding capacity of the nursery area and the duration of the feeding season and in the south of England many will smolt at one year old. In the Highlands of Scotland the majority migrate when they are three years old whereas in the Scandinavian countries they could be as old as five years. In the autumn before smolting parr from the head waters of rivers often move further downstream to be better placed for migration the following spring. But the main downstream movement begins in the spring time and shoals of smolts can be seen dropping quickly down the river system between March and June. They move downstream tail first for the most part but do swim head first for short distances mainly in the slower running water. As they migrate they feed voraciously and are once again easy prey for the trout fishers' lures. At this stage they are extremely sensitive to handling and the silver guane coat which they have adorned to protect their scales and skin from the erosion of salt water is not yet hardened, therefore, when the trout fisher handles them to remove the hook if he handles them carelessly he will remove much of this coating and if he does, even though they are not harmed by the hook-hold they will perish once they reach the sea. There is little doubt that once again due to ignorance many smolts, which are by now quite sizeable, are kept by anglers.

The Ph value of the feeding tributaries is a very important factor regarding the productivity of these areas. A feeding area with a value over 7 compared with a feeding area with a value of 5 is rather like comparing a rich arable farm with marginal arable land, this is due to the range of invertebrates that can survive in differing Ph values. A Ph value of 4.5 is the lowest value that is acceptable to salmonoids and they cannot survive in Ph's lower than that figure.

Forestry planting on headwaters can be largely responsible for lowering the Ph of streams running through these plantations and especially in the case of spruce plantations Ph values can be lowered from the range of 7 to as little as 3.2. Forests planted close to waterways once they have grown over 8 feet begin to form a close canopy which shields the sunlight from these watercourses. The result of this is that algae which relies on sunlight to promote its growth becomes retarded. The invertebrates which fish feed on in turn rely on the algal growth to provide feeding, therefore, they diminish in numbers.

Land and forestry drainage very often create erosion to banks and beds of burns and these watercourses therefore become torrential and unstable, once again this continual movement of gravel down these systems acts rather like a pan-scrubber and prevents algal growth becoming established.

Once the smolts have descended the river system and enter the estuary they pause for a short space of time in order to acclimatise themselves to the drastic change in specific gravity between fresh and salt water before heading out into the sea and oceans beyond to the rich feeding grounds far from our shores.

There is little doubt that once the smolt enters the sea he feeds very voraciously. He quickly grows feeding teeth sharp as a razor and preys on all sizes of smaller fish and other foods such as plankton all of which vary tremendously in size according to the water temperature of the seas that he travels through and feeds in. Most of the smolts which will grow into salmon travel to an extensive feeding ground between the coast of Newfoundland and Greenland where they remain for two or more sea winters. However, the smolts that will return as grilse do not travel so far as they only spend one sea winter in the sea. The difference between a salmon and a grilse is just that the latter spends only one sea winter in salt water. They are both fully matured fish and the common belief that a grilse is a young salmon not fully mature that will return the following year as a salmon is a complete myth.

Once these creatures become mature the urge to regenerate the species makes them once again begin their homeward migration to fresh water and the rivers that they were born and bred in. As they approach their homeland they lose their feeding teeth and stop feeding.

It is thought that the main migration of salmon returning to the United Kingdom approaches the area of the Outer Hebrides. Those coming to our northern and eastern rivers swing up past the Butt of Lewis through the Pentland Firth and then a large proportion of them swing down the North Sea and turn in to land opposite the Yorkshire coast before facing the ebb tide and as they follow the coastline north funnel into their respective rivers. Fish homing to the north coast rivers and rivers north of the Moray Firth funnel into their rivers as

Leaping salmon at the Cassley Falls, Ross-shire

they pass them. The majority of fish going to the west coast rivers and the south coast rivers of the country, swing in past Barra Head into the Irish Sea and then the channel to enter their rivers of origin.

There are four main runs of fish, the winter, spring, summer and autumn runs which virtually overlap each other, each run lasting approximately three months. Not all rivers can accommodate the four runs of salmon as the stock of a salmon river is firstly almost entirely controlled by the amount of spawning gravel available in the river system and secondly by the feeding capacity of the nursery streams, tributaries and the main river. If either of these commodities are overcrowded it is to the detriment of the stock of these rivers and in all cases the earlier runs of fish will suffer. This is the main reason why the short west coast rivers only have a summer run of fish and the smaller north and east coast rivers for the most part have only two runs, the spring and summer runs. In actual fact there is only one river in the British Isles that can accommodate the four runs and that is the river with the largest catchment area, namely the Tay.

Salmon return to fresh water for the sole purpose of reproduction and their main objective having entered fresh water is to ascend to the approximate area in the river system where they themselves were produced. Spawning times vary considerably throughout the country according to the time when the salmon enter the river and the altitude of the river systems.

In the early part of the year water temperature largely controls the speed at which salmon are able to ascend the river system as it is physically impossible for them to ascend weirs, fast rapids and more formidable falls when the water is below certain temperatures. Depending on the form and size of the obstruction they have to ascend, salmon can be stopped if the water temperature is between 38–52°F. Above 52°F salmon are able to ascend any ascendable obstruction unless water conditions are unfavourable. And in the case of some falls fish are only able to ascend over quite a narrow range of water height.

Once the fish have ascended to the proximity of their spawning areas they remain in the nearest holding pool to the spawning area until they become ripe to spawn.

When they have spawned the salmon becomes known as a kelt, this also applies to grilse and very shortly after spawning 90% of both salmon and grilse male kelts die. A smaller number of females will also die after spawning but the rest of the female species either return to the sea shortly after spawning during high water conditions, while others remain in the river system up till March or April before finally descending to the sea.

It is normally reckoned that approximately 40% of the females return to the sea and that approximately half of these will return to spawn a second time and a very small proportion a third time. It is, however, reckoned that the number that return to spawn a second or third time only constitutes about 2½% of the total stock of a salmon river. The second return fish are easily recognised in the early part of the season because they have fresh water maggots in their gills and also a very distinguishable purple blotch about the size of a shilling, on the gill casing. A second return fish can be often found with gill maggots and sea lice and salmon second returns are normally 12 lbs and upwards in weight.

Female fish that through some disability have not been able to spawn are known either as baggots or rawners whereas the male is known as a kipper.